Access and use of Grey Literature in Social Science : Problems and Prospects

Access and use of Grey Literature in Social Science : Problems and Prospects

Rama Devi Tella

Ess Ess Publications

4837/24, Ansari Road, Darya Ganj,
New Delhi-110002
✆ : 23260807
Fax : 23274173
E-mail: info@essessreference.com
url:http://www.essessreference.com

First Published **2006**

ISBN: 81-7000-486-1

Rs.395/-

Published by:
Ess Ess Publications
4837/24, Ansari Road, Darya Ganj, New Delhi-110 002
Tel: 011-23260807, 41563444 Fax: 011-41563334
E-mail: info@essessreference.com
url: www.essessreference.com

Printed in India at:
Printline, New Delhi

DEDICATED TO MY BELOVED PARENTS and IN-LAWS.

Who encouraged for my professional development

Late. Sri. Satyanarayana Murthy Deverapalli (Father)

Smt. Veeravathi, D (Mother)

Late. Sri Subba Rao, Tella (Father-In-Law)

Smt. Laxmi Kanthamma, Tella,

Ex MP and MLA (Mother-in-Law)

Sri Satyanarayana Tella (Father-In-Law)

Smt. Pramoda, Tella (Mother-In-Law

FORWARD

Containers of Knowledge are many. The print revolution after the invention of the movable type of Johann Gutenbury in the fifteenth Century the paper replaced the earlier containers of knowledge such as the Clay tablets, Papyrus rolls, Parchments and other types of manuscript copying materials. Over the last five centuries the vehicles of knowledge changed from paper to computer. The print culture brought to the forefront the formats of Book and Periodical. There are also other publications other than books and periodicals which started to appear in Special libraries and Academic Libraries. Such publications generally include the Reports, Pamphlets, Theses, Dissertations, Patents, Standards, Conference Papers, Preprints, Off-prints, Occasional papers, Committee and Commission Reports, In-House papers, Maps, Trade Literature, Leaflets, Posters, Pictures etc. which cannot be arranged on the shelves of the library. These items are collected apart from the library's main collection. These micro-literature found sometimes more important than the macro-publications like books and periodicals. It is not the containers but the content of documents has become important. During the period of information explosion such micro-documents increased in each library and caused a number of problems. There is no generally accepted term which describes such literature, although various names have been applied from time to time. Finally the expression "Grey Literature' has come to stay.

The 'Grey Literature' plays an important part in any special library and collectively, these documents form one of the librarians most valuable resources. There is no universally accepted definition for the 'Grey Literature' though there are many definitions. *Harrod's Librarians Italy Glossary* explains the term Grey Literature as "Semi-Published" material, for example, reports, internal documents, not formally published or available commercially, and consequently difficult to trace bibliographically. There are many problems in tracing, acquiring and arranging the Grey Literature in Libraries. With the advent of documentation and computerization the arrangement of these spineless and less visible materials are causing less headaches to libraries and library staff. It is, however, found that there is a need to have a network of the libraries having these materials at the national level to cross over the problems of access. In advanced countries we come across such networks like BRIT (British Reports, Transactions and Theses) and SIGLE (System for Information and Grey Literature in Europe) etc.

Dr.Rama Devi during her service at the NIRD has abundant experience and interaction with the faculty, Research Scholars and participants and realized the importance of 'Grey Literature' for the preparation of their 'Survey Reports' and project works. Etc. The NIRD also established a National Documentation Centre named as "Centre On rural Documentation" (CORD). Dr.Rama Devi conducted a study on Use pattern of GL and presented a paper at an International Conference on GL at Washington, DC, USA in 1999. This background inspired Dr.Rama Devi to take up research on Grey Literature for her Ph.D. Very few people have worked in India on this theme. Not much literature is available on this subject. In spite of many inherent barriers, she worked on the subject sincerely and efficiently. Dr.Rama Devi is a dynamic LIS professional with varied experience in special libraries. She, therefore, could do justice to the subject.

Dr.Rama Devi proposed a national network for Grey Literature available in India with the following objectives:

a) To improve the detection, identification and collection of grey literature available in India.

b) To provide access and delivery of each document available in the Database, and

c) To set up an Indian bibliographical Database of Grey Literature and make it accessible through Internet

This volume on Grey Literature is helpful to find the nature and problems relating to the arrangement of Grey Literature in libraries. It is useful to LIS teachers, students and scholars and deserves to be in all libraries especially in special libraries and Academic Libraries. Dr.Rama Devi is known to me as an efficient and intelligent professional for the last two decades. I feel is a great honor to write the preface to this excellent piece of work and wish the author success in her endeavours

'Sankranti'
14.1.2006

L.S.Ramaiah
University Librarian (retd)
Hyderabad
Ramesh Mohan Library
CIEFL, Hyderabad

Contents

List of Tables

List of Figures

List of Abbrevations

ADB	Asian Development Bank
AGRIDOC	Agricultural/Information and Documentation
AGRIS	Agricultural Research Information System
ANGRAU	Acharya N.G. Ranga Agricultural University
ASCI	Administrative Staff College of India
ASLIB	Association for Information Management
BAIF	Bharatiya agro-Industries Foundation
BLLD	British Library Lending Division
CAG	Comptroller and Auditor General
CALIBNET	Calcutta Library Network
CAS	Current Awareness Services
CDB	Centralised Data Base
CDROM	Compact Disk Read only Memory
CDS	Centre for Development Studies
CEACS	Centro de Estudios Avanzados en Ciencias Sociales
CESS	Center for Economics and Social Sciences
CIRDAP	Center for Integrated Rural Development for Africa and the Pacific
CLIC	Computerised Library and Information Clearinghouse
CORD	Center on Rural Documentation
CSIR	Council for Scientific and Industrial Research
DDB	Distributed Data Base
DELNET	Delhi Library Network
DEVSIS	Development Science Information System
DOE	Department of Electronics

DTP	Desk Top Publishing
EAGLE	European Association for Grey Literature Exploitation
ESCAP	Economic and Social Commission for Asia and the Pacific
FTP	File Transfer Protocol
GILS	Government Information Locations
GLIS	Grey Literature Information Systems
IATUL	International Association of Technical University
ICPE	International Center for Public Enterprises
ICSSR	Indian Council of Social Science Research
IDPAD	Indo-Dutch Programme on Alternative Development
IDRC	International Development Research Center
IFLA	International Federation of Library Associations and Institutions
ILC	International Law Commission
ILO	International Labour Organisation
INDEV	India Development
INFLIBNET	Information Library Network
INFROSS	Information requirements of the Social Sciences
INIS	International Nuclear Information System
IPE	Institute of Public Enterprises
IRMA	Institute of Rural Management, Anand
ISEC	Institute of Social and Economic Change
IT	Information Technology
JRD	Journal of Rural Development
LAN	Local Area Network
LRDC	land Research Development Center
MANAGE	National institute of Agricultural Extension and Management

MIDS	Madras Institute of Development Studies
MoU	Memorandum of Understanding
NABARD	National Bank for Agricultural and Rural Development
NASSDOC	National Social Science Documentation Center
NGO	Non Governmental Organisation
NIC	National Informatics Center
NICNET	National Informatics Center Network
NIN	National Institute of Nutrition
NIR	National Institute of Development Research and Documentation
NISIET	National Institute of Small Industries Extension Training
NRSA	National Remote Sensing Agency
NTIS	National Technical Information system
ODA	Overseas Development Agency
OECD	Organisation For European Economic Development
OU	Osmania University
PIDSA	Population Information and Documentation System for Africa
PIS	Pre – Investment studies
SCOP	Standing Conference of public Enterprises
SDI	Selective Dissemination of Information
SIGLE	System for Information on Grey Literature in Europe
SIRD	State Institute of Rural Development
SOSIG	Social Science Information Gateway Technology
UAP	Universal Availability of Publication
UBC	Universal Bibliographic Control
UGC	Union Grants Commission
UNDP	United Nations Development Programme

UNESCO	United Nations Economic Social and Cultural Organisation
UNICEF	United Nations Children's Fund
UNISIST	Universal System for Information in Science and Technology
UOH	University Of Hyderabad
URL	Uniform Resource Locator
WHO	World Health Organisation

1
Introduction

1.1 Information

We are living in an information age / society. It means that skills acquired in the application of information to solve problems is the key to material gains and progress. The production and techniques of communication of information have been witnessing revolutionary changes as information is a fundamental resource for national development and the progress of individual. Information is one of the important basic needs of human being. It is an essential input for every organization when it is used for purposes such as decision making, problem solving. Information is vital for scientific and economic progress. Both as a body of facts or ideas as well as a message endowed with response potential, information is a key input in the process of achieving behaviour modification of the individual and social development. Free access to information is a social right, and individuals and communities are entitled to have easy and free access to information. Public information is the social memory and constitutes the information world. Information generation is an unending process like evolution.

The information is transferred from one person to another person from one place to another place through various communication channels. They are oral, written or print media and now the electronic media.

1.2 Oral Sources

Oral communication is limited to smaller and restricted groups. It may take place between one to one, one to many, many to one and many to many. The oral sources may consist of (1). Conversations; (2). Group Discussions; (3). Seminars / Conferences/Workshops; and (4). Invisible colleges.

1.2.1Conversation: People during their leisure hours at home, in offices or during their morning or evening walks pass on information involuntarily among themselves. This can happen even in office corridor talks.

1.2.2Group discussion: This is another informal source of information. Groups of scientists, engineers, research scholars, teachers, students, etc, discuss informally about their work in progress. Group discussion is a recognized source of information.

1.2.3 Seminars/conferences/workshops: They are yet another sources of information. Discussions at seminars, conferences and workshops are often on particular themes or subject area(s). On these occasions various people come into contact with each other and during their personal discussions exchange information which is otherwise not available.

1.2.4Invisible colleges: Peers in various subject fields or managers of organizations or institutions, etc. can form invisible colleges. Information before it can take a formal form passed on among the members of the invisible college . Latest data, results, innovations etc. are exchanged freely amongst the members.

1.3 Incunabula

All the documents of the pre-Gutenberg era were hand written documents using various formats such as bricks, skins, vellum, papyrus, Bhurjva patras and Talapatras, metals, cloth and paper. They are known as incunabula.

1.4 Printed sources

One of the most significant event in the history of mankind was the invention of movable type in the 15th century by John Gutenberg. From the 15th century onward, there has been a flood of printed matter resulting in an affluence of recorded information. The printed sources consist of books, periodicals, pamphlets, reports, theses, standards, patents, trade literature, proceedings etc. The volume of these materials is doubling every 10 or 15 years. The printed sources enabled man to overcome the limitations of space and time in information dissemination. Internet made the information transfer much more faster and convenient. Consequently, the problem of searching for information has become a serious concern for library and information professionals. The knowledge of various information sources will help the librarian to develop effective collection development policy.

1.5 Information Resources

There are two broad categories of information sources namely Documentary sources and Non-Documentary sources. The documentary sources may be categorized as "Primary Secondary and Tertiary "sources of information. The primary sources are the first published records of original research and development. Primary sources are most important for research. They help the researcher to keep himself up - to - date and well informed of the latest developments. By its nature, the primary literature is widely scattered, and it is difficult to locate it. The original reports of scientific and technical investigation from the bulk of primary sources. Some of these records are reports of experiments containing findings and conclusions.

Not all documents are generated through research. Many documents are the by-products of other activities. For example, a government department records its activities every year and the outcome is the Annual Report of the department.

1.6 Social Sciences

Social sciences constitute a branch of human sciences. Here, man is the object of research. It may well be noted, however, that the specific character of this object entails a certain number of consequences. Man is not studied exactly in the same manner as a physical object, or a plant, or an animal. Amongst all human sciences, social sciences are distinct from natural disciplines which study physical aspects of man like medicine, or which consider men as individuals like

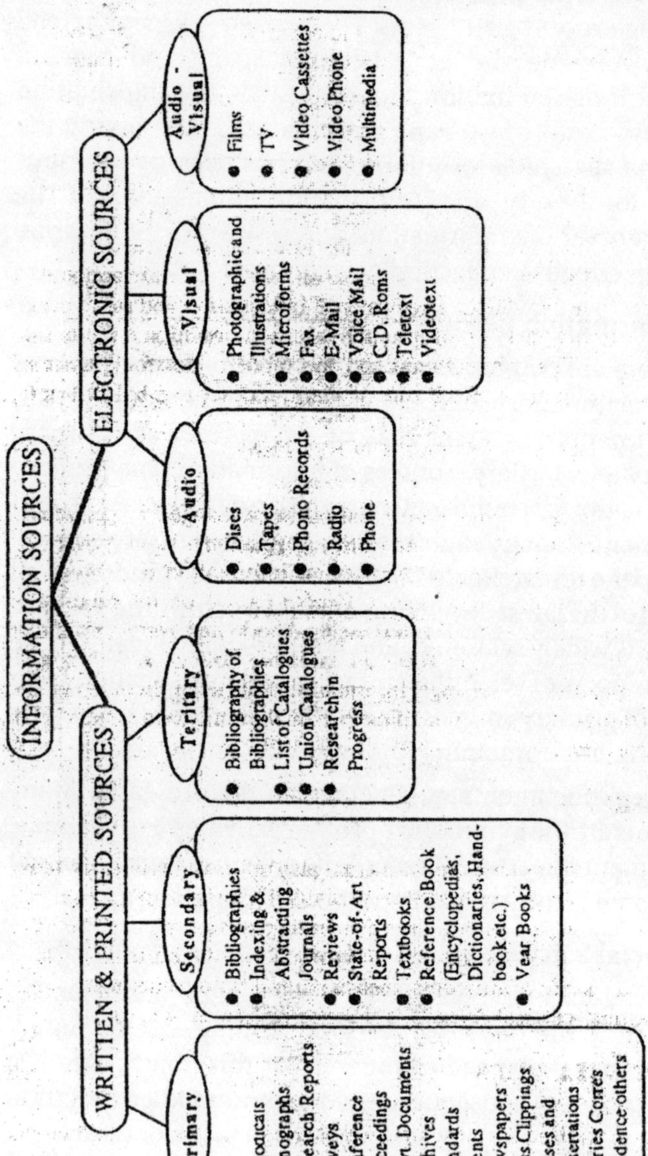

Kinds of The Written, The Printed and The Electronic Source of Information

psychology. Social sciences study a particular category of human phenomena: social phenomena, social facts.

In an initial observation, we may define social facts as those that result from social life. and, as such, would not find place in a completely solitary human existence. This is also true, for example, of language created in order to communicate with others. Social facts are, therefore, facts concerning man living in society.

However Social Sciences are not clearly definable area according to Moris Line (1971) and Stephen Roberts (1976) and are defined differently in different countries and individual social sciences are interpreted quite differently.

1.7 Grey Literature

The word 'Grey' has an element of ambiguity in its characteristic. Any grey area generally refers to an aspect, situation or topic that does not fit into a particular category and is therefore difficult to deal with. Grey Literature (GL) has been variously described as fugitive, unpublished, invisible, non-conventional, ephemeral, informal and not commercially available literature (IDRC,1975). And it is also difficult for bibliographic access. The non-conventional document is physically large, produced for a small group of uses and distributed free or under exchange agreements. It is frequently not traced by documentation services including commercial ones.

Grey literature is a type of informal communication, which on a scale of formality, fits in somewhere between conversation and normal publication. A formal publication may follow later but in many cases contrary to the common assumption these papers may not be made publicly available at all. Nevertheless, grey publications may contain comprehensive, concrete and up-to-date information on research findings, and investigations have shown, that even when they are published officially at a later stage, detailed information on techniques, methods, measured values and details of experiments are frequently omitted. These details are important for further research, and the non-conventional literature is then becomes the first and only source of information.

1.7.1 Coverage of Grey Literature : Grey Literature covers all segments of knowledge. It serves the information needs of various people from different disciplines. It is important that researchers in all the fields, planners, policy makers, consultants and even educationists, keep themselves up-to-date with the latest developments and be aware of work carried out by others in their fields. A significant proportion of such information is available only in the form of semi published or non-conventional literature. Such an information is, many a times far more detailed than what appears in the conventional literature and is generally available much earlier before a journal article or book is published.

The range of topics, covered by GL is enormous and very often it discusses topics at micro levels. The authors of GL or the corporate bodies which produce GL operate at all levels of academics, business, industry, scientific research and social groups. The quick dissemination of information is the primary concern to both the producers of GL and the end users. Therefore, it functions as an important link in the total information transfer.

1.7.2 Types of Grey Literature : Several varieties of GL can be identified, such as preprints, working papers/occasional papers, conference proceedings (if not published) theses/dissertations, all types of reports- like project reports, feasibility study reports, market research reports, Committees and Commission reports, statistical reports, annual reports, research reports etc.. All government publications, training manuals/course material, lecture notes, technical notes, memoranda, house journals/Newsletters, Pamphlets/booklets, brochures, trade literature, supplementary material, backup documents etc.

1.7.3 Availability of GL : In India several institutions, government laboratories, bodies like CSIR, ICSSR, Government departments, public sector undertakings, universities are producing, maintaining and disseminating information in the form of GL. There is a wealth of potentially useful, relevant and much needed locally generated information as grey literature but there are barriers to its access and availability due to poor knowledge of its existence, poor bibliographical control, underestimation of its value, lack of information policy for GL, budgetary constraints are some of the problems associated with GL.

It is very difficult to make any estimate of output of GL. The DEVSIS (Development Science Information System) study report of 1975, co-sponsored by IDRC, ILO, OECD,UN Department of Economic and Social Affairs, UNDP and UNESCO, was an important first step in a comprehensive manner to inform about defining GL, identifying the difficulties in obtaining and make available GL in any given situation. DEVSIS study team divided information sources into two major categories namely the visible and invisible. Visible here refers to the published materials (books and serials) and invisible refers to the unpublished materials. The team concluded that out of the world's information resources, 40% was published and 60% was unpublished, (less accessible, grey, fugitive, unpublished working papers, feasibility studies, consultancy reports, theses, research reports, government documents and documents of international organisations and which are not widely disseminated).

1.8 Need for the Study

The term "exponential growth of literature" or "literature/ knowledge explosion" had been conventionally enunciated with "open", "formal" or published documents with the exclusion of unpublished documents or "non-formal" ones like technical reports, project feasibility reports, dissertations and working papers.

According to the DEVSIS study report, 60% of the literature in social sciences is grey, out of these how much literature is known to the users, how much is accessible and available to the social scientists and how to make more efforts to enhance its utility are the issues frequently addressed in the context of GL. However, there are very few studies showing the value of GL and the acquisition and dissemination of such type of literature . In this context, there is a need to study the awareness level of the social scientists, about the existence of GL, and to know how much importance the social scientists are giving for the GL in their day to day activities, in the work environment, exploring the ways and means for enhancing the availability and usage of GL. Internet as a source of information in the present context of IT also needs to be evaluated. Hence the present study is undertaken to examine the above issues in detail pertaining to GL.

1.9 Statement of the Problem

Social sciences cover many disciplines like Anthropology, Economics, Sociology, Education, Politics and History. All these subjects are interlinked with one another and influence the life of the human beings. The social scientists should keep themselves abreast of the latest knowledge in their area of specialisation. Also social science researchers need specific data which varies from place to place and society to society.

Review of literature revealed that so far use of GL by social scientists has not been highlighted as it is considered to be one of the major sources of information in social science research and bibliographical control is one of the barriers for its accessibility, availability and use. The present study, therefore, is undertaken with the following specific objectives.

1.10 Objectives

1. To study the awareness, accessibility and use of grey literature by the social scientists
2. To study the acquisition, organisation and dissemination of grey literature by the social science libraries
3. To identify the barriers in accessing grey literature.
4. To examine the potential of Information Technology as a tool to access the grey literature.

5. To prepare a model for bibliographical control and sharing of information on and about grey literature.

1.11 Hypothesis

Whether there is significant difference in the perceptions of the respondents with reference to GL documents (in terms of relative preferences).

1.12 Methodology

As it is difficult to assess the use of GL by social scientists of all the social science institutions in India, the scope of the present study has been narrowed down to cover the important social science institutions in Hyderabad in Andhra Pradesh

A pilot study was conducted to test the questionnaire and modified some questions removing the ambiguity if any in the questions to the respondents and to obtain qualitative and quantitative information.

CHART A

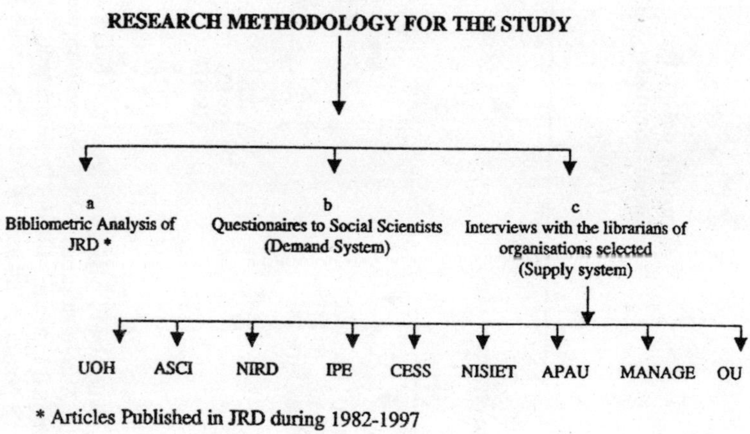

Fig 2.

CHART B

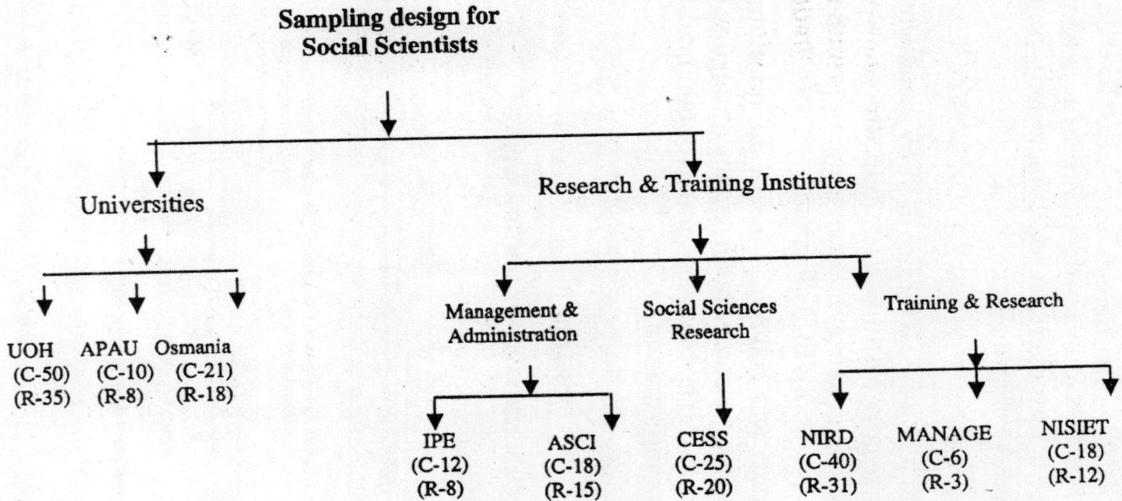

C=Contacted
R-Received

UOH=University Of Hyderabad ; ANGRAU=Acharya N.G.Ranga Agricultural University; OU=Osmania University Campus; IPE=Institute of Public Administration; ASCI=Administrative Stafff College of India; CESS=Centre for Economic and Social Sciences; NIRD=National Institute of Rural Development; MANAGE=National Institute of Agricultural Extension and Management; NISIET= National Institute of Small Industries Extension Training.

Multistage stratified sampling technique was used to select the respondents. The researcher identified the Institutions/Departments who are dealing with social sciences. The identified institutions were further classified into Universities/Academic, Research and Training Institutions and exclusively working on social science research activities. The researcher interacted and distributed a questionnaire to the librarians of the selected institutions to know their views on the topic.

To examine the first objective viz., to study the awareness, accessibility and use of GL by the social scientists, the indicators like (1) sources to know the existence of GL (2) purpose and use of GL (3) personal collection development (4) membership in professional associations (5) attendance in number of conferences in an year and (6) bibliometric analysis (7) awareness about the organisations who are publishing GL on an regular basis and (8) priority- wise use of GL documents by the social scientists were analyzed in detail.

In order to study the second objective i.e., to study the acquisition, organisation and dissemination of GL by the social science libraries ,the researcher used the variables like (1) acquisition policy (2) methods of procurement (3) dissemination methods like CAS and SDI (4) organisation of GL material (5) type of arrangement in the libraries etc. To identify the barriers in accessing GL (one of the objective), the researcher examined the constraints like (1) lack of bibliographical control (2) Lack of awareness (3) Lack of accessibility (4) lack of availability and (5) Organisational defficiency.

To examine the fourth objective that information technology as a tool to access the GL, the researcher gathered the data on (1) internet use (2) material available on internet (3) awareness about networks and different databases etc. Finally to examine the objective of preparing a model for Grey Literature Information System (GLIS) the indicators like (1) social scientists views about the networking of institutions (2) need for a separate database on GL documents (3)

Establishment of separate information system for GL etc., were made use of. Based on the ideas given by the social scientists the researcher proposed a model for GLIS, which was discussed in detail in the Fifth chapter.

1.13 Limitations

In any study dealing with information which is not always sufficient to satisfy the total needs of all the user groups, it is difficult to generalise the findings. This difficulty gets further accentuated in a study which is largely exploratory in nature. Adding to this, the usual deficiencies of survey research make one to be circumspect about the results, inspite of the care taken with regard to sampling methodology.

Also non availability of sufficient number of documents in the Indian context, with reference to the GL and its various dimensions is another limitation felt by the researcher.

Though the GL information system proposed is to encumpass a wide variety of organisations in the country, the present study is limited to the social science research and training organisations located in Hyderabad, Andhra Pradesh.

1.14 Chapter Plan

The study has been divided into six chapters including introduction and conclusion in addition to the appendices.

In the introduction, information, concept and sources, subjects covered by social sciences, grey literature, need for the study, statement of the problem, objectives, hypothesis, methodology including limitations have been discussed.

The second chapter deals with the social sciences its growth and development, role of ICSSR, social science information gathering agencies, information seeking behavior of social scientists. INFROSS study etc.

In the third chapter, the concept of GL, factors responsible for growth of GL, special characteristics of GL, attitudes of librarians towards GL, GL and internet, future of GL in networked environment and user education and GL etc. were out lined. Grey Literature and its formats were included in the Fourth chapter

The analysis of the data obtained through a questionnaire administere to a cross section of users of GL is presented in detain in the Fifth chapter. The data gives an insight into the user profiles apart from their views about the demand system of GL and the problems faced by the users. It has also analyzed the views of the librarians in order to meet the demands of the users.

Based on the analysis in the fifth chapter, a Grey Literature Information System was proposed in the Sixth Chapter comprising of nine institutions in social sciences in Hyderabad. The design of the proposed system is also elaborated with the activities and facilities for the participants .

In the seventh and the last chapter the researcher included the suggestions received from the respondents based on their qualitative and quantitative responses, followed by the conclusions drawn from the study .

1.15 References

Aina, L.O (1987) : Grey Literature in Agricultural Research in Nigeria. *Quarterly Bulletin of the International Association of Agricultural Librarians and Documentalists*, 32(1), 48-50p.

AlberaniVilma, De Castro Pietrangeli Paola, Rossi Mazza Anna Maria (1990) : The use of Grey Literature in health sciences: A preliminary survey.*Bull.Med.Libr.Assoc.*,78(4), 358-363p.

Allison, P (1987) : Stalking the elusive GL.:*College and Research Libraries News*, 48 (5) May, 244-246 p.

Ambrose, D.P (1984) : The collection and bibliographic control of grey literature of Lesotho (Mimeo) Amesterdam : North-Holland.

Artus, H.M (84) : GL as a medium for scientific communication. *Journal of documentation, 35 (3), 139-141p.*

Auger, C.P (1998) : Information sources in grey literature. 4th ed. London : Bowker- Saur, 177p.

Chillag, J. (1982) : Non-Conventional literature in agriculture- an overview. *IAALD quarterly Bulletin*, 27(1), 2-7p.

Dbachere, M.C (1995) : Problems in obtaining Grey Literature. *IFLA Journal*, 21 (2), 94-98p.

DEVSIS (1976) : The Preliminary design of an international information system for the development science. Ottawa : IDRC.

Gelfand, J.M (1998) : Teaching and exposing Grey Literature : What the information profession needs to know, examples from the sciences collection building, 17 (4),159-66p.

Hanada, T (1984) : Grey Literature, its variety and problems. *Journal of Information Processing and Management*, 27(7),595-602p.

Hayashi, S (1998) : Grey Literature in Japan. *Pharmaceutical Library Bulletin*, 43(3), 277-83p.

Holland, M (1989) : Times past and times to come : the world wide activities of research publications serials, 2(1), 49-50p.

Howard, T.W. (1993) : Electronic Distribution of Hypermedia on Wide-Area Networking Systems : An Update. *Technical Communication. /third quarter*, 438-448p.

International Development Research Centre : DEVSIS (1975) : The preliminary design of an international information system for the development science. Ottawa:IDRC, 247p.

Keriguy, J (1984) : Acess to Grey Literature : the contribution of the CNRS Centre for Scientific and Technical Documentation. *Bulletin-des-Bibliotheques-de-France*, 29 (2), 138-143p.

Kwafo-Akoto, K. (1988) : Acquiring unpublished population documents in Africa : A personal experience. *ASLIB proceedings*, 40 (4), 105-110p.

Levin, M.A (1989) : The grey ghetto : Key issues related to public policy research literature. *Collection Building*, 10(1-2), 29.33p.

Line, M B. (1971) : The Information uses and needs of Social Scientists : An overview of INFROSS. *Aslib proceedings*, 23, 166-171 p.

Luzi, D and Molinas, P (1987) : AGRIS, INIS, COSAT, SIGLE. *Bulletin of Information*, 27 (3-4), 325-344p.

Mainieri, R (1987) : Grey Literature in the Italian ministries : Production, bibliographical control and availability. *Bulletin of Information* ,27 (3-4), 415-421p.

Norton, T (1983) : Grey Literature. *State Librarian* ,31(2), 16-17p.

Palnikov, M.S, (1989) : Small circulation (Grey) literature in the institute of information in social sciences of the USSR. Academy of Sciences. *Inter lending and Document Supply*, 17(1) ,16-19p.

Peach, M (1998) : Archiving the internet web pages of political parties. *Assignation* ,15 (4) ,8-54p.

Posnett, N.W and Baulkwill, W.J. (1982) : Working with Non-conventional literature. *Journal of Information Science*, Vol 5, 121-130p.

Raseroka, H.K (1986) : Relevant library services in developing countries. *IFLA Journal*, 12(4), 288-291p.

Rathapo, S.B (1998) : Grey Literature on Women and Gender in Botswana. *Information Development*, 14 (3), 144-51p.

Roberts, Stepen (1976) : The size, growth and composition of social science literature. *International Social Science Journal*, 28 (1) .

Schidmaier, D. (1986) : Ask no questions and you will be told no lies: or how we can remove people's fear of "Grey Literature". *Libri*, 36(2),98-112p.

Thorpe, P (1985) : Priorities in information management for strengthening National Agricultural research. *Association of Agricultural Libraries and Documentalists*, 30 (4), 77-84p.

Thielemann, J. (1986) : Grey official publications. *Bibliotek* 53(2),88-90p.

Tyagi, K.G. (1999) : Information support Development studies. DESIDOC. *Bulletin of Information Technology*, 18(4), 9-19p.

Van-der-Meer, K (1987) : The future of information resources for science and technology and the role of the library, 157-164p. (edited by Nancy, Sweden, IATUL).

Vender Heij (1985): Synopsis publishing for improving the accessibility of grey scholarly. *Journal of Information Science*, 11, 95-107p.

Wood, David. (1982) : The role of British Library Lending Division. *Aslib proceedings*, 34 (11/12, 459-65p.

2
Social Sciences: Growth and Development

2.1 Introduction

Social sciences are an authentic body of classified knowledge of human society formulated with the objective of discovering general truths or the operation of general laws. Within the scope of definition, the social sciences can justly lay claim to being called sciences.

New Century Dictionary defines 'social science or sciences as the science or group of sciences concerned with all that relates to the social condition of man, or to his existence and well-being as a member of an organised community".

Macmillan Modern Dictionary defines social sciences as "science which treats the structure and development of society; sociology, also any group of studies dealing with man in his relation to his fellow beings and his environment, as geography, civics, economics and history".

According to Encyclopaedia Britannica, the social sciences are concerned with orderly investigation of the behaviour of man in society with the aim of cumulating a body of relevant theory. Theories concerning group behaviour, whether economic, political, social are legion. They are implicit in men's actions, transmitted in customary beliefs and elaborated in literature".

Webster's Third New International Dictionary defines social sciences "as the branches of knowledge that deal with the institutions and functioning of human society, and with the interpersonal relationship of individuals as members of society".

According to Charles A. Beard (1934), " social science is a body of knowledge and thought pertaining to human affairs as distinguished from sticks, stones, stars and physical objects'. He further stated that they are concerned with the actualities of human societies in development with thought and with methods of acquiring knowledge respecting their actualities of human societies in development.'

According to E.S.R.A. Seligman (1957), "Social Sciences be defined as those mental or cultural sciences which deal with activities of the individual as a member of group. Thus social sciences are concerned with the disciplines that deal with human behaviour in its social and cultural aspects - economics, political science, sociology, social and cultural anthropology, Social psychology, social and economic geography.

White's (1973) Sources of Information in the Social Sciences includes history, geography, economics and business administration, sociology, anthropology, psychology, education and political science as the main subjects of social sciences. These subjects have, in common, a concern for the behaviour of man in relation to his fellows and to the environment they share.

The Indian Council of Social Science Research (ICSSR) has laid down, for the purpose of research support, the following subjects as constituting social sciences: anthropology, commerce, demography, economics, education, geography, law, management, political science (including international affairs), psychology, public administration, sociology, statistics, town and country planning, etc. History is excluded as this is covered by humanities. Indian Council of Historical Research takes care of historical studies. Social history could be considered a social science as it studies the social aspects of the human history.

2.2 Disciplines Covered by Social Science Institutions

Eugene Garfield's(1985) observation that the scientists of the Third World countries (particularly India) are engaged more in those areas of scientific research with which they are not immediately concerned, indicates that Indian scientists are busy with a highly technical research which India can ill-afford. His observation may or may not be applicable in the field of social science, but two things are absolutely clear: (i) that Indian scientists are second to none, and (ii) that high technical research is not a monopoly of the developed countries alone.

New social science subjects are emerging because of the tremendous research activities going on in the traditional as well as the non-traditional subjects resulting in a flood of literature in various forms and formats. The U.N. and its agencies specially UNESCO have contributed a lot to the growth of social science literature through its missions and units. After Second World War, a large amount of literature relating to poverty, illiteracy and hunger, etc., has been produced by UN and its agencies . These are common problems faced by the Third World countries.

Most of the Indian social science institutions and universities reflect similar approach regarding the coverage of disciplines. Economics, sociology, anthropology, education, geography, political science, psychology, statistics, history, management, etc., are quite popular social science subjects. Library science, population studies, oriental studies, agricultural economics and rural development, science and technology, health care and family welfare, journalism, American studies, environmental science, banking and public finance, biographies, art and culture, social linguistics, computer science are comparatively new subjects and are developing fast. The subject of management developed during the last few decades has become an important branch of social science study.

"It was under the impact of British rule that social science thinking first emerged in India"-this is how an average Indian social scientist reacts to the appearance of social sciences on the Indian scene. But this remark is tangentially true. The perspective of the total Indian society and culture should be taken into consideration in tracing the development of social sciences.

Gupta (1972), an eminent Indian sociologist, in his famous treatise provides a gist of the 'primary accumulation' of social sciences in India. This work is liberally drawn upon in the account that follows. This backdrop should enable particularly the librarians and other information providers to appreciate the range of sources of social science information on India.

2.3 Development of Social Sciences in India

Scholarship and libraries have been in existence in India since time immemorial. Indian civilization is one of the oldest in the world, dating back to 3000 B.C. In ancient times, India was the centre of institutions of higher learning . Libraries were a part of the Indus Valley Civilization which flourished in India from 2000-1500 B.C They were called 'pustakalayas' and the collection in these libraries consisted of inscribed cylinder seals and clay tablets. Confirming the tradition of learning and teaching in India during ancient times, Dr. S. Radhakrishnan once said: 'In the old days teachers of India were themselves librarians and they were held in very high esteem".' It is believed that knowledge passed from one generation to another by way of oral teaching. The handwritten books were few and were considered a rare entity worth preserving for future generations. Social sciences were claimed to be a part of India's heritage.

Social sciences in their development are viewed as relatively young in comparison to the natural sciences . The ideas of social sciences developed from philosophy as did many other branches of knowledge. Now they have an independent status of their own and after a long period of neglect, they have gained recognition. Systematic study of various aspects of human society which began in the 19th century has expanded further in the 20th century, and vast piles of information have accumulated in each of the disciplines of social sciences. As a consequence of this accelerated activity, the subject matter of social sciences is divided, and divided again, forming new, more specialized sub-disciplines. Among the subjects which formed social sciences, two main tendencies dominated: first was to drive towards unification, i.e. towards a single master social science, the second was to drive towards diversification. The latter triumphed with the result that highly specialized disciplines have emerged.

During the British rule, development of social sciences in India was slow because the system of higher education was narrowly conceived and was not conducive to serious academic work. Also social science studies during this period were, narrowly confined to the decennial censuses and surveys started by the British Government in the seventies of the 19th century, and ethnographic studies of Christian Missionaries who did missionary work in the tribal areas. Slow growth of social sciences during the colonial rule could also be attributed to the fact that many Indian universities did not offer facilities for doctoral work. But the dawn of independence and the expansion of the university system have greatly stimulated the growth of social sciences.

2.4 Planned Development in Post-Independent India

Immediately after 1947, the Government of India found itself facing many social and economic problems. On the one hand, it was busy handling the havoc created by the partition, and on the other, it had the country's completely shattered economy staring in its face. In the circumstances the National Government first thought of adopting planned economy through Five Year Plans. So the Planning Commission was set up in the year 1951. It was entrusted with the work of systematic economic planning with fixed targets. Although the targets were always short of expectations, they did wonderfully well to meet the priorities of the nation. For example, the First Five Year Plan (1952-55) gave importance to the improvement of national income; Second Five Year Plan to industrialization (1957-61); Third Five Year Plan to fertilizers, power generation, etc., (1962-66); Fourth Five Year Plan to complete those incomplete projects to yield immediate results (1969-74); Fifth Five Year Plan (1974-

79) accorded top priority to projects capable of yielding results in the short run; Sixth Five Year Plan (1979-84) to rural development; Seventh Five Year Plan (1985-90) gave top priority to agriculture, employment generation and increase in productivity. Eighth five year plan 1992-97 gave priority to Human development and the Ninth plan 1997-2002 is encouraging private initiative and investment.

2.5 ICSSR and the Social Scientists

The emergence of the Indian Council of Social Science Research (ICSSR) in the late sixties is the most significant event in the annals of social sciences development in the country. The Council has been mainly responsible for the policy-formulation, promotion and financing of social science research in this country, since its establishment.

The Indian Council of Social Science Research came to be established on 15th April, 1969, under the Ministry of Education and Youth Services. Dr. D. R. Gadgil and Shri J. P. Naik, both distinguished social scientists, were appointed as the first Chairman and the Member Secretary respectively of the Council.

2.5.1 Objectives of ICSSR : The main objectives of the Council are (a) To review the progress of social science research and to give advice to the users in government or outside. (b) To sponsor social science research programmes as well as research projects. (c) To provide technical assistance for the formulation of social science research programmes. (d) To coordinate research activities. (e) To develop and support centres for documentation. Service maintenance and supply of data, inventory of current social science research and preparation of a national register of social scientists; (f) To organise, sponsor and finance seminars, workshops, study circles, working groups/parties, and conferences for promoting research or utilisation of social science research. (g) To give grants for publication of social science research work, and to undertake publication of digests, periodicals and journals devoted to such research; (h) To institute and administer scholarships, fellowships and awards for social science research etc.

2.6 Growth of Social Science Research in India

2.6.1 Rapid Increase in the Number of Universities after Independence : In 1947, there were about 70 universities. In 1975-76 the number of universities rose to 101. Today there are nearly 300 universities and are deemed to be university institutions in the country. In 1971, 91 universities had 823 post-graduate departments in social science subjects out of which 397 were located in universities and 426 in colleges affiliated to the universities. The number of such departments has been growing with qualified and competent faculty, which have been responsible for the growth of social science literature.

Development of social sciences can be assessed by the number of universities and colleges, university departments, research institutions, number of doctorates in social sciences and by the establishment of RPC, UGC, ICSSR themselves. The Association of Indian Universities has brought out a bibliography of doctoral dissertations of social sciences, which presents the development of social sciences. More than 1,000 doctoral theses in social sciences are submitted to the Indian universities every year.

2.6.2 Emergence of Funding Agencies for Research in Social Sciences : Prior to independence, development of social science research was inexorably linked with the growth of universities and research institutions only. The government apparently did not play any active role in the propagation of social science research. But the establishment of the Planning Commission in 1950 gave impetus for the involvement of the government in social science research. The Planning Commission after its creation realized the need for social science research on the topics of relevance and significance for national development. With the establishment of UGC and ICSSR, the promotion of social science research was given the needed impetus, thus a firm foundation for the development of social science research was laid. ICSSR and UGC have offered grants to universities and social science research institutions for promoting research.

Among the foreign agencies, the United States Educational Foundation in India (USEFI), the Ford Foundation and the Rockefeller Foundation have been providing financial assistance for social science research. Among the private Indian foundations, mention may be made of the Tatas, Birlas and other industrial and business families and companies. But the government is the main funding agency for social science research. In the distribution of funds for research, however, social sciences are given a low priority.

2.7 Social Science Information Generating Agencies

The following areas/sectors are considered as the major social science information generating agencies.

(a) State agencies such as the legislature, executive and judiciary in addition temporary organs of the state, such as commissions, panels and working groups, are constituted from time to time to advise the government on matters where it is considered advisable to seek such advice;

(b) Institutions, for example, universities, college departments, research and documentation centres, organisations of the trade, industry and labour, associations of professional persons, etc.;

(c) Individual research and resource personnel and the corporations and companies

(d) International agencies such as the U.N. and its allied agencies, the World Bank and its associates and transnational corporations and

(c) Foreign organizations and individual research workers working on socioeconomic and political problems of the countries other than their own."

The information generated by the above-listed agencies is contained in files, data documents, committee and commission reports, trade and institutional publications, Research reports and Ph.D. dissertations, etc. It is clear from statistics that the social science monograph production is increasing year after year although compared to science and technology, monograph production is not that high.

India's monograph production during 1970 was 4,979 titles, 4.6 per cent of the world total, and it ranks seventh. Surprisingly, India also ranks seventh in serial publications.

It is estimated that about 100,000 documents are produced annually by the U.N. and its affiliated agencies alone. There has been remarkable growth in the serial production dealing with social sciences. Also Ulrich and Unesco estimated the number of social science serials at between 20,000 and 27,000 titles in 1970.

According to the Checklist of Social Sciences Serials (CLOSS) there were nearly 4,000 current titles in 1974. This includes academic titles only. In 1820, the number of current serials was just 22. In 1920 the number rose to 694. In 1950, it rose to 1806, in 1961 to 2251 and in 1970 rose to 3490. This surely shows tremendous growth of social science.

Government agencies are not only important generating agencies for social science information, but are potential users of such information appearing in various monographs, research reports, surveys and other documents. Therefore, for an effective utilization of social science information, bibliographical control is necessary. Also in-order to bring discipline in the prevailing chaotic state of affairs.

2.8 Social Science Information Gateway (S0SIG)

The Social Science Information Gateway (S0SIG) allows social science researchers and practioners easily to discover and access relevant high-quality networked resources and services world-wide including data archives and statistical software. It also provides a comprehensive list of relevant UK based sources. SOSIG points to hundreds of resources on subjects ranging from Anthropology to Statistics. All the resources that appear on the gateway have been catalogued and described to aid users. Users can access SOSIG at the URL http://sosig.ac.uk. It can be also accessed through telnet to:

Sosig.ac.uk

Login as: sosig

2.9 Bibliographical Control

Bibliographical control is a concept as well as a system of adequate recording of published/unpublished and audio-visual material through which one knows about their existence. It is necessary to have a cheek over the tremendous proliferation of publications so as to know their whereabouts and make its effective use. Various attempts have been made at the national and international level. Most significant of these are by UNESCO, IFLA and SOSIG. The UNISIST programme inquired into the feasibility of a world science information system including social sciences. The UPA programme was meant for improving national and international provisions for supply of documents and was jointly launched by UNESCO and IFLA.

Under 'Delivery of Book Act, the Government of India has made it compulsory for the publishing trade and the institutions, organisations and individuals to deliver books at four libraries in the four metros. The Indian National Bibliography is supposed to cover the publications to bring them under bibliographic control. Current national bibliographies have been in vogue for long, as a system of copyright publications by national governments. Retrospective national bibliographies have also been found useful for evaluating the rich national literacy heritage.

2.10 Information seeking behaviour of social scientists

Almost all the user studies conducted in the initial stages related to the field of science and technology. When Paisley (1966), for instance, made an attempt to review user studies in social sciences in 1965, he concluded that there was no literature to review! But, in 1968, Alien (1969) maintained, "The number of studies concerned with social and behavioral scientists has become quite large in the past three years and is growing at a prodigious rate." However, this claim was disputed by Brittain (1970) who concluded that the number of studies in social sciences is still very small.

Even where a few user studies in social sciences were conducted, they drew heavily upon user studies in sciences for guidance on methodological issues. The methods of enquiry of science user studies continued to be applied without much modification to the social sciences, even though it had been established by 1960s that the fundamental differences between the scientists, and social scientists made the methods of user studies in the one, inappropriate in the other.

The differences between sciences and social sciences in the context of information approach were further highlighted by Line (1968), who enumerated 12 ways in which both tended to be at variance with each other:

(i) The subject matter of the social science is less stable than that of the sciences;

(ii) There are many types of approaches, and it is not unusual (as it is in science) for a researcher to question the whole validity of a given approach.

(iii) Methodological disputes are much common in the social sciences;

(iv) Each discipline in the social sciences is much less clearly defined than in the sciences.

(v) the scatter of potential relevant information is much greater in the social sciences than in most sciences.

(vi) the relevance of information is harder to assess in the social sciences.

(vii) the social factual content is probably quantitatively less than that in the sciences and is almost certainly less vitally important

(viii) concepts and ideas are more important in the social sciences

(ix) the unstable subject content and the strong conceptual element in the social sciences tend to make identification of information requirements difficult

(x) the nature of discovery in the social sciences is a different phenomenon from discovery in the sciences

(xi) scientific information is superseded by subsequent discoveries and general laws but there is no agreement that this takes place in social sciences; and

(xii) the pattern of research may be quite different in social sciences.

Line's (1971) analysis, which he himself termed as working hypothesis, was a prolegomena to an extensive empirical investigation under- taken at the Bath University during 1968-1970.

2.11 Bath University Experiment/INFROSS Study.

The Investigation into Information Requirements of the Social Sciences (INFROSS), carried out at the University of Bath between 1968 and 1970 was the largest survey of its kind to date. As Skelton (1973) puts it, one of the reasons behind the project was the fear that in the absence of knowledge about information requirements in the social sciences, solutions adopted in sciences, based on the findings of science user studies, would be applied in the social sciences.

The findings of the Investigation revealed that though both the groups (the scientists and the social scientists) by and large use similar information sources, similar methods to retrieve information, and both experience similar problems in dealing with the information, yet the extent of use of different methods and the degree of problems created do vary and account for the differences in the information seeking behaviour of scientists and social scientists. These differences, as reported by Skeltan (1973), relate to the behavioural factors described below.

2.11.1 Sources of Information : The greatest demand for information made by scientists is for the archival collections of serial publications, supplemented by unpublished reports and a variety of informal contacts and interchanges. The scientist is primarily concerned with obtaining information about the research activities of other scientists, the results of the research, and theoretical and conceptual developments. In social sciences, data that is generated by researchers themselves forms only a small proportion of the information required by social scientists. As a matter of fact, some of the types of data may be generated and collected outside the confines of the social science disciplines (e.g. institutional data, historical archives, court records, tax returns, school records, birth and death records, prison records etc.) for purposes unrelated to social science research. The Investigation findings revealed that while social scientists use both monographs and journal literature, scientists lean slightly more heavily on journal literature. Theses and research reports are not considered particularly useful by scientists and social scientists. Citations, abstracting and indexing journals are used both by the social scientists and the scientists, though social scientists prefer to use separately published bibliographies. Neither scientists nor social scientists find reviews particularly useful for locating information.

2.11.2 Methods for Retrieving Information : While the social scientists depend to a large extent on the formal system of communication, such as the library and the reading material available therein, scientists do not consider library information services as particularly useful. Informal communication, including 'invisible colleges play a large part in research activities of the scientists.

2.11.3 Information Use : In social sciences, users look for paradigms that match their interest for a particular subject of enquiry. They need considerable opportunities to browse and to cover a wide range of literature-both conventional and unconventional. The user in sciences needs primarily the standard texts; he will not have the same requirement for access to the most recent research and he will not be interested in unconventional literature.

2.11.4 Attendance at Conferences : Similar percentages of scientists and social scientists attend conferences. However, the social scientists value conferences not so much for the papers presented as for the information gained through personal contact.

2.11.5 Delegation of Literature Search : Majority of the social scientists conduct their own research, while scientists prefer to delegate it to specialized information officers.

2.11.6 Linguistic Ability : Linguistic ability of social scientists is generally less than that of scientists. Perhaps the reason is that social science is more concerned with local circumstances dictated by culture, whereas science is more international.

If social sciences are environment bound, as has been pointed out above, then the obvious inference is that the concerns of social scientists in the developing countries are not the same as those of their counterparts in the developed countries. This inference is equally applicable to their information seeking behaviour as well.

The Third World countries should pay more attention to their own social science research and documentation, and rather less to that of the industrialized countries. According to Britain (1985) the principal argument here is that most social science research is not international, in the sense that the findings do not travel well across language and cultural boundaries. This is partly because of the different social, economic and psychological problems from one country to another, and partly because the methods that may be appropriate for the study of social science problems in one country are not necessarily the most appropriate in another. The extent to which social scientists make use of their own social science material differentiates one country from another, and also one social science discipline from another.

Information providers in the developing countries should, therefore, develop their own methods in support of their social science research and writing. It is partly the above exhortation and partly, but more importantly, the present author's own conviction that studies of the information seeking behaviour of Indian social scientists must be conducted in the Indian setting .

The third chapter is discussing fully about the Grey Literature, concept, definition, features, characteristics, bibliographical control, accessibility and availability role Of internet in its accessibility etc. This information may pave the way for subsequent discussions in other chapters in highlighting the importance of Grey Literature in the social science information chain, especially in Indian setting.

2.12 References

Alien, T.J (1969) : Information needs and uses. *Annual Review of Information Science and Technology, Volume* 4, 3-29p.

Beard, Charles A (1934) : Nature of Social Sciences. New York : Charles Scribner.

Britain, J.M and S.A. Roberts (1976) : Information Sources in the social sciences:Development and Rationalization. *International Social Science Journal*, 28(4),835-40p.

Garfield, E (1985) : Society's unmet information needs. *Bulletin of the American Society for Information Science*, Volume 12,6-7p.

Gupta, B.D (1972) : Sociology in India. Centre for Sociological Research, Report no11, 1-22p.

Line, M.B (1968) : Social Scientists Information. *Social Science Research News Letter*, 3,2-5p.

Paisley, W (1966) : Information needs and uses. *A Review of Information Science and Technology*, Volume 3, 1-30p.

Seligman Edwin, R.A (1957) : what are social sciences ? Encyclopaedia of the social sciences. New York : Macmillan, 1,3-7p.

Skelton, Barbara. (1973) : Scientists and Social Scientists as Information Users : A Comparison of results of science Users studies with the Investigation into Information requirements of the Social sciences. *Journal of Librarianship*, 5 (2),138-156p.

3
Concept, Characteristics and Control of Grey Literature

3.1 Introduction

Grey Literature (GL) covers all segments of knowledge. It serves the information needs of various people from different disciplines. The word 'Grey' has an element of ambiguity in its characteristic. Any grey area generally refers to an aspect, situation or topic that does not fit into a particular category and is therefore difficult to deal with.

It is important that researchers in all the fields, planners, policy makers, consultants and even educationists, keep themselves up to date with the latest developments and be aware of work carried out by others in their field. The authors of GL or the corporate bodies which produce GL operate at all levels of academics, business, industry, scientific research and social groups. The quick dissemination of information is the primary concern to both- the producers of GL and the end users. Therefore, it functions as an important link in the total information transfer. For the three players of the game GL means generators, organizers, and users, it is more work load, more details to be aware of, more money to spend for production and delivery ,less possibilities to get revenues, less possibilities to achieve a lean production organization and less priority.

Recently, an increasing number of documents are published on the world-wide web and can therefore be easily accessed if the web address is known . Unfortunately as with printed grey publications, such electronic documents are also difficult to detect.

3.2 Colour Codes for Identification of G.L

Use of colour codes to identify literature is an accepted practice. There are blue prints of engineering drawings and architect plans. The advertisements that are printed in telephone directory for products and services are called yellow pages. The official government documents are known as white papers.

Auger (1998) has defined use of different colours in different countries. In the United States, the word "Blue Book" is used to denote various official publications, especially the state manuals which give biographical and other details about government employees. In France, the colours are yellow and white. In Germany, the government documents are white while in Italy, it is green and in Belgium, it is grey.

Different categories of material are covered by the concept of GL. Moreover, they are in different sizes, formats and in almost all subjects. This very peculiar nature of the documents make them stand between black and white as belonging to the GL varieties.

3.3 Pink literature

Literature is talked about in terms of grey. One can view information that is not accessible as being black and fully accessible information as being white. The color analogy was applied to information being purposely withheld because of security, privacy, or classification reasons. For information that does not fall in a legally withheld (red) category, but it is not released (white). The genre of pink information was recently created. This bit of levity points to an information that may present acquisition difficulties.

3.4 Grey and White

The following table shows the difference between the 'grey' and 'white'. (Owen, J.M, 1997)

Table 1. Difference between Grey and White

	GREY	WHITE
Relative Volume	Increasing	Decreasing
Speed of production and delivery	High	Low
Cost of information	Low, decreasing	High, increasing
Accessibility	Limited, restricted	Global, Unrestricted
Quality control	To be provided by innovative technology	Organised through traditional peer review process
Long-term archiving	Problematic due to volume and technological ageing	Problematic due to legal restrictions and technological ageing
Role of libraries	Loss of traditional roles opportunities for new services	Limited by legal restrictions
Role of publishers	Marginal, limited to support functions	Diminishing

3.5 GL in Different Subject Areas.

G.L varies in extent from one scientific discipline to another, and therefore also from library to library. Regarding certain types of libraries i.e special libraries. GL tends more to white, while with others i.e public libraries it tends to dark Grey

3.6 Factors Responsible for Growth of GL

1. Rapid development of universe of knowledge
2. Modern methods of copying
3. Telecommunication

Whenever concern is expressed at the continually increasing quantity of GL, and at the difficulty it presents to librarians, information workers and documentation experts on the one hand, and to readers and users on the other, the reply which is often given is that such publications are not intended to form part of the permanent literature, and consequently any problems that may arise will be purely temporary. Unfortunately, this sanguine view is belied by the overwhelming evidence of the durability of GL and by its frequent citation in library catalogues, bibliographies and reading lists of all kinds. Those who prepare and issue GL do so because such documents offer a number of advantages over other means of dissemination, including greater speed, greater flexibility and the opportunity to go into considerable detail if necessary. Another important reason why GL has attained significance as a separate medium of communication is because of an initial need for security or confidentiality classifications which prevent documents from being published in the conventional manner.

Over the years, GL has come to constitute a section of publications ranking in importance with journals, books, serials and specifications, this importance is now achieving the recognition it deserves and GL is no longer the Cindrella of information sources. Any subjective feelings that GL is being used and quoted more and more are borne out by the many independent references to it, and by the emergence of databases devoted specifically to standardizing its definition and improving its accessibility. Lim (1975) estimated that over 70% of the World's agricultural literature is unpublished.

The Land Resource Development Centre (LRDC), USA library's annual intake shows that 65% of the monographic material can be described as non-conventional 50% of the Soil science material can be termed as non-conventional, it has been raising to 75% for natural sciences. It is surprising that the majority of agricultural experts feel that much knowledge and latest information will never appear in any other form except as GL.

3.7 Production

Levels of production of GL changes from one discipline to other and, in one discipline itself, it varies depending on typologies. In information sciences, Alberani y De Castro have concluded 22.1% shile making an analysis of most significant journal references, where 1377 were GL. In physics a 6% of the references were GL. (12,335 references of a 39,000 references).

In social sciences, based on SIGLE databases, Michael Kluck made a study from 1984 to 1993 where it is shown that, of the total number of documents in SIGLE(412.572 documents) a 29%(121.334 documents) were social sciences documents. A study was also made in DIALOG databases. Out of 274 databases, 74 of them (31.6%) contains grey information. It depends too on topics in social sciences. It is about a 30% or lower in other disciplines. In every study done about this, reports, proceedings, theses, etc. were the most looked up documents.

An important part of scientific materials are made up with this kind of literature and is increasing constantly. For example, the growth-rate of scientific articles produced in USA in the last 15 years is about 40% while the growth -rate of grey materials, managed by NTIS (National Technical Information Service) is about 400%.

3.8 Grey Literature Producing Agencies

Bodies which typically issue GL include : 1. Associations 2. Churches 3. Libraries 4. Museums 5. Educational establishments 6. Federations 7. Government departments 8. Institutions 9. Laboratories 10. Pressure groups 11. Private publishers 12. Research establishments 13. Societies 14. Trade Unions 15. Trusts and 16. Universities. Such bodies have a standing invitation to contribute their publications to the collection centre which is being built up at the British Library Document Supply Centre. Some bodies make available regular lists of new publications and invite direct applications for copies of recent documents. Others publicise their offerings in catalogues and indexes prepared by a variety of organizations willing to act as selling agents or distribution points.

It is difficult to identify all producers of GL. The first step forward is to have an inventory of actual and potential producers of GL within each country. Having identified the producers it will be necessary to sensitize them on the need to deposit at least a copy of their publications to a designated depository centre within each country. In addition, each producer should be encouraged to maintain a textual data bank of all their publications as well as a bibliographic database of all their publications which they can make available to their actual and potential users.

3.9 Special Characteristics of GL

Some of the main characterstics of grey literature areas as follows.

1. They tend to have rather specialised subject content or concentrate on subjects of only local interest.
2. Their specialised subject content or parochial limitation often renders them unattractive for publication in conventional forms.
3. They, therefore, tend to be issued in rather limited editions or small print runs. This often results in their being issued in mimeographed format.
4. Their non-conventional formats result in non-uniform or variable standards of editing and production.
5. Their non-uniform standards and unattractive forms make effective pricing, and marketing difficult
6. The difficulty in pricing often results in their being distributed at no cost, an obvious advantage to poorly funded libraries in most developing developing countries
7. Thc limited editions also result in poor availability, limited accessibility, poor distribution, poor publicity and ultimately, poor bibliographical control.
8. Their poor bibligraphic control can perhaps be attributed to their failure to provide bibliographic details like the imprint (place, publisher and year of publication), or the International Standard Book Number)
9. Also because of their poor bibligraphic control their output is difficult to estimate since they can emerge from the least expected sources, both institutional and individual, and are issued and distributed in a rather haphazard manner.

10. Their bibliographic control defies the concept of Universal Bibliographic Control(UBC) and consequently they make the idea of Universal Availability of Publications(UAP) seem an elusive mirage.
11. The question of non-uniform standards of production raises issues like the size, usually only a few pages, which makes them liable to be viewed as trivia.
12. If they get issued in non-paper media like microfilm or electronic media, they raise even more complex issues of compatibility, and they require special equipment to make them usable. The very fundamental issue as to whether they could or should be acceptable in manuscript form would require addressing.
13. The advent of desktop publishing (DTP) has also boosted the ease and rate of production of GL and has helped in improving the quality of production
14. The difficulties associated with their identification, collection and use, make them unattractive and complex to control.

The above features of GL which are by no means exhaustive, create situation of ambivalence. It is ironical that even though libraries in developing countries lack foreign currency to procure the foreign literature which may not bear direct relevance to their local situations, they tend rather to look down on their own local GL which they can usually obtain free of charge. This attitude of libraries in developing countries may be attributed to a variety of causes. One of these causes has been attributed to what has been termed the "made in there" syndrome, one of the typical vestiges of the colonial legacy, whereby practically everything produced locally is considered inferior in comparison to the imported type. Admittedly, books produced in the developed countries have a high standard of production, are more acceptable internationally and also command greater authority eventhough they are a great deal more expensive.

Aside from the subjective cause, there are also the clearly

demonstrable negative features of GL generally, as already identified above. There is the general line of thinking that it is the unattractiveness, limited runs, poor and non-uniform standards of production, poor editing, small size, poor distribution and accessibility that make local GL tend to be undervalued by librarians in developing countries. Here also it must be admitted that even if they were attractively produced, some GL, for the reasons already given, do not create a strong enough attraction anyway.

3.10 Attitude of Libraries towards GL

Lukewarm attitude of libraries in developing countries towards GL arises from the fact that most librarians tend to concentrate on books and journals and fail to have a broad perspective of other information resources. This arises from the traditional book oriented attitude of many librarians in developing countries.

Arising from the physical features and even the specialised content of GL, libraries in developing countries, because of their limited personnel in terms of both quantity and in cataloguing skills, as well as the general lack of expertise in handling such special material, the subject content of which may not be adequately catered for in the various classification schedules, or the cataloguing of which makes greater demands on the cataloguer, librarians are often not inclined keen to handle such material..

The flimsy or physical characteristics of GL also demand special storage equipment and facilities like pamphlet boxes or filing cabinets which are an additional drain on the limited financial resources of libraries in developing countries. These libraries also have to contend with the issue of conservation arising from the poor durability of most GL which are often produced on poor quality paper, in mimeographed form, and in simple binding using metal staple pins.

An important contributory factor to the indifferent attitude of libraries of developing countries to GL arises from their generally weak publishing and book development industries. The weak infrastructure for a thriving book industry also partly contributed to the proliferation of GL in many developing countries.

GL has always had a role in academic research but the attitude of librarians apparently is not that encouraging, Why? . Because it is not easy to collect nor control. In hunting and gathering of GL material, librarians see themselves as collectors or acquisitions agents, and organizers to make information available and then preservers for future generations. It usually requires additional expertise and time to process, describe and classify. It does not come from traditional sources, nor get it automatically nor experience adequate demand for it. As such, librarians do not practice an aggressive approach for collecting GL either. Instead they are reactive, satisfying demands that are more likely to be induced through Internet. This new wave of access to GL has opened a Pandora's box.

What we have seen in the last 3-5 years is a startling proliferation of finding aids to help librarians and users in the commercial identification of such materials and more specialised directories of laboratories, centres, think tanks, consultancies conducting sponsored and independent research and developing new spin-off technologies and products that the public has an interest in. Traditional GL frequently ends up in "office grey" physical vertical file cabinets and librarians dislike that because they can't maintain it appropriately, and it requires special care and curatorial management to effectively retrieve anything from it. It takes valued in libraries which have no room to expand as is and suffers from a high degree of lack of comfort in use. Microform was once a substitute, now replaced by low use CDROM titles. Controlled subject access is difficult to assure unless subject thesaurus construction becomes a priority and that tends to require major commitments from the librarian.

3.11 Grey Literature and the Internet

The Internet, which sprang from the organisations and institutions which have long been producers of GL, appears to have had two main impacts on the world of reports and other unpublished documents. Firstly, the internet is being seen as a means of disseminating GL, and especially fugitive literature, and secondly the network has been used enthusiastically by grey literature providers and coordinators to publicize their activities and services. The internet has also proved a convenient medium for bodies of outsiders. Apart from what may be termed problems of quality control, the material available via the internet is also frequently laborious to access with long searches likely to run up considerable phone bills, especially of downloading times if included as well. The advent of Internet has inevitably prompted a great deal of rethinking among workers active in the grey literature field and many aspects are currently being examined and evaluated.

3.12 New Forms of Grey Literature

Usually the GL is unprocessed papers and folders, obscure works and most recently downloads of database files. Some of the GL that has become increasingly visible of late contains even the archives of television programmmes and news releases, where if missed at the time of programming, it is not easily retrievable and available for later viewing and study unless some repository or archive of such material is committed to retaining it.

New forms of communications, in grey literature refer generally to material which is not systematically published or readily available. Much of this information is being packaged in evolving formats and systems. There are many conferences and task forces addressing the issues of how to manage or find material in the new networked world. Commercial publishers are actively trying to understand their future in view of these changing conditions. Non- technical issues, copyright being one of the most critical ones, are being hotly debated. As noted in a recent article by

T.W Howard (1993) " One of the major problems associated with electronic publishing on internet has been the lack of a centralized distribution mechanism. Until recently, trying to find a particular file at an FTP site has been a bit like looking for a particular book in the library of congress without the benefit of a card catalog."

The evolution of enabling technologies, where potentially much greater information is freely available, has resulted in a situation where more information can now be considered grey or difficult to find and not easily accessible through normal channels. The irony of the information age is not a problem of scarcity, but of overload.

Grey information or GL of the 1990s is a phenomenon of sifting through the masses of data to find the right information at the right time, especially when it's all out there available. The challenge of identification and cataloging of technical reports in the 1960s is now reincarnated as a challenge of navigating through LISTSERVs, bulletin boards, FTP sites, and with know-bots, Government Information Locators(GILS), Gopher Servers, Archie, World-Wide Web, Veronica etc. These last few creatures are new forms of location or identification tools, a new approach to "Bibliographic control" of the new GL. The question of GL here is whether traditional definitions still hold or do we need to rethink our approach to difficult to access material in a networked world. At a minimum it is clear that we have added an interesting time dimension to the world of GL. This is something that always existed in databases that were updated. However, because of the Internet, the new kind of communication it enables, as well as real time publishing and distribution that is taking place today, this problem is generally exacerbated and the volume and diversity of grey information needs are greatly increased.

3.13 The Future of Grey Literature in Networked Environment

The amount of documents available through electronic networks is increasing in a spectacular fashion. In future, more and more organizations will use the network as a distribution channel for their publications. Increasingly, the problem of GL will become a problem of networked publications. What we should try to do, now that GL is moving into the era of networked publishing, is to create an infrastructure, which provides at least a similar level of control and access. There are two benefits in doing so. First, the value of GL to society will be greatly enhanced. Second, networked publishing will become an attractive and cost-effective alternative to traditional publishing. The networked publishing will lead to much higher level of use of many publications which we now think of as 'GL . If networked dissemination of institutional publications is organized well, access to such information will become much easier. Dissemination will become more rapid. Information acquired will be re-usable. Feedback to the author will be easy. These are all things that can enhance the value and usefulness of GL. This will all lead to an increased role of GL in relation to official publications. The networked publishing can have an impact on both the producers and the users of GL. People involved in GL have a more important responsibility, which is to make the potential value of GL available to society. They should use information technology to do just that. Therefore, the strategy to be followed is to stimulate the use of electronic networks for the distribution of GL by the organisations that produce such literature. That strategy will increase the value of GL.

The network is also a means for obtaining all kinds of published and unpublished information. In many ways and increasingly so in years to come the network is becoming a substitute for traditional information media such as published journals, libraries and online databases.

3.14 Bibliographical Description of GL

Since GL appeared, the problem of description is known: There are two pressure groups in the last 40 years that influenced the description of the non conventional literature and established basic rules: COSATI and INIS. The COSATI rules were adopted by many US databases including GL and by the INIS system, which itself became strong in the seventies and international databases were not only organised according to this model, but used its rules too.

Implementing the relevant ISO-standards and the mentioned rules for bibliographic description by all partners in the chain from production to usage of GL could bring them together. It is true that a report published with all elements described and an exact bibliographic description means more work and therefore costs more money. But if they are used, it is cost- effective, because all partners could use the information in the same way. It is cost-effective, because literature not used for information exchange is very expensive and also the work has to be done only once and can be used again and again.

3.15 Consolidation of GL

Much has been achieved in establishing and promoting announcement services, databases and national collections of GL. To take just two examples, in the case of the British Library Document Supply Centre, the collection includes 3.62 million reports in microform, 450,000 other reports, 440,000 US doctoral theses, 100,00 UK doctoral theses, 314,000 conference proceedings, over 539,000 translations, and 25,600 items of local authority material. Acquisitions are announced in British Reports Translations and Theses and details, as already noted, sent on to SIGLE. Detailed discussion about SIGLE was discussed in chapter 5th

In Hanover, the Technische Informations Bibliothek has a large collection of GL available through the TIBQUICK service, notably 900,000 dissertations and reports from the USA, 180,000 German dissertations, 83,000 unpublished German reports, over 100,000 translations, 200,000 volumes of conference proceedings, and 190,000 papers and preprints. Acquisitions are announced in Forschungsberichte, and again details are supplied to SIGLE. Thus GL is readily available and it is well-documented and yet an adjective often applied to it is "difficult to ask for", difficult to identify, and difficult to get hold of. The criticism of "difficult to ask for" is particularly well justified, for whilst a request can never be as simple as please supply a copy of Hard Times by Charles Dickens, 1845. Some of the identifiers currently in use of GL are not easily quoted, especially over the telephone, and even when written down, can often lead to transcription errors.

3.16 Themes in the Access and Management of GL

a) **GL is easier to describe than it is to define:** A number of speakers at the Fourth International Conference on GL at Washington D.C (1999) gave definitions of GL. However, most of the definitions were based on some of the characteristics of GL for example, it was difficult to locate and was not published through regular commercial channels. It was also pointed out that gray information may be different from GL. Grey information may be the more significant concept in terms of user needs. The term literature is instructive since the phrase and its association with being gray comes from the documentalists' or librarians' sense that it is not under effective bibliographic control and, once identified, cannot be easily obtained in a traditional documentation format. In today's technological environment, the concept of gray information in new forms and are used here as they were at the conference, interchangeably and with a lack of precision regarding how and why they are used differently. This is perhaps a point bearing further consideration and research.

b) **Free information Versus Freely Available Information:** The theme that information being freely available is not the same as free information was significant for improving access to GL, especially in the context of government information. In the U.S many believe that government information should be free. Implicit in this assumption is that free means free to the public since the taxpayers, already are paying to develop, package and disseminate GL. To the extent that agencies cannot charge for information, are not funded for public dissemination activities, or unable to put a price tag on the activities, resources for getting this information packaged for dissemination are constrained. To the extent that information is recognised as having a cost and this cost is factored into making information available, more gray information will become more easily accessible, not only through government channels, but also through the public/private interface.

c) **One person's GL is another person's white papers :** Another point with regard to networking and interpersonal communication was that one group's GL may be another group's white papers. A particular case in point was made when the head of publications at an international organisation described the publication process and access tools of that organization. In fact, documents were available through regular, if not commercial mechanisms. The information from that organisation was unknown to some of the audience and therefore viewed as gray. Once the system was explained, the same audience viewed the material as more accessible and, therefore, less gray. In a more general sense, libraries, database producers, information brokers, end users all have their own standard sources for information and these are not considered gray. However, when one tries to trace another's sources, they venture into what might seem gray areas to them. GL can also vary by the subject field. Science communities differ in this regard. For example, preprints are a standard format for exchange in high energy physics and these are controlled through preprint management systems within the community. Biologists, on the other hand, would not consider sending out preprints broadly for fear of insulting colleagues or being scooped.

3.17 Obsolescence

The period for which GL should be retained as part of a store of information will vary with local conditions and requirements. Any policy will have to take into account the actual use made of the material, the availability of archive copies in collections elsewhere, and the collection's own role (if any) as an archive source itself . The employment of microforms considerably eases the problem of storage and security, as does the digitization of texts to create digital images for online use and possible CD publication. GL has not been around long enough as a distinct category to have given rise to many studies as to its obsolescence rates, whereas in the technical reports area a number of attempts have been made to determine how long publications can usefully be retained. In particular, high rates of obsolescence were noted in a study by Wilson (1964) at the Atomic Energy Research Establishment, and much more recently by Vickers and Wood (1982) who were moved to say that it has been repeatedly mentioned that the demand for GL collected by the (British Library) Lending Division is very low. Whilst a lack of awareness of the value of GL is without question one factor, obsolescence or perceived obsolescence could well be another .

3.18 Acquisition of GL

GL can be obtained on a routine basis by a variety of methods, but two of the most commonly used are 1. Exchange agreements with other organizations, if permitted, 2. Purchases by subscription or on a single item order basis .GL in the third world is produced for a specific purpose. In this regard, only limited copies are made to be distributed to specific people. In the case of annual reports for instance, the materials may be confined to decision and policy makers in the government machinery. The producers rarely think of commercializing the literature. Furthermore, such literature may be restricted from public consumption. Some organisations may produce limited copies on account of financial and other economic constraints.

3.19 Factors Responsible for Inaccessibility of GL

Many factors militate against organising and disseminating GL. The prominent ones being the so called confidentiality of GL, low perception of GL and the lack of infrastructures to support the bibliographic control of GL.

Another important factor is the lack of infrastructures to support bibliographic control of GL. Most countries have national libraries which are empowered by law to have all publications emanating within each country to be deposited with the national library. The library is thus expected to publish anually a national bibliography which will invariably include GL every year. Publishers and authors are mandated to deposit their publications with the national library of each country but this is hardly the case and no sanction is made against them. Hence only a fraction of producers do deposit their publications with national libraries. Many countries have stopped publishing national bibliographies, and those that do, are many years behind schedule like in India. Even within various organisations, as earlier reported, only very few of them can produce a list of their publications. This is also true of researchers and scholars who attend conferences and workshops. Once proceedings of such workshops and conferences are not published, the writers may never locate such papers physically. (Aina, L O, 1993)

3.20 User Education and GL

User education about the importance of GL in his work, its various forms, awareness, access and availability etc would facilitate better appreciation of the problems involved. At first the potential user must be informed about, which GL is available where and how he can use it. For the user only the available information sources are those he can see i.e.,(1) in bookshops (2) exhibitions (3) Professional friends and colleagues (4) through the advertisements in the mass media and technical literature (5) in the form of reviews.

Advanced users can be introduced to (1) the information systems which offer GL predominantly 2. bibliographies & abstract journals which offer GL and 3. particular categories of GL e.g., reports, conference literature, business documents, patents etc. As the user is the decider about which of the tools he should make use for awareness and accessibility and its ultimate use, the researcher went about collecting the data in its various facets by designing an appropriate questionnaire.

The researcher collected primary data through

questionnaires from the social scientists and librarians of the selected organisations. Analysed the data and drawn some conclusions about the awareness, accessibility, availability and use of GL. Also collected secondary data from the Journal of Rural Development (JRD) citation analysis in order to assess the use of GL in the field Rural Development as it is considered to be a major interdisciplinary subject in social sciences. The coverage of GL in JRD was compared with the coverage of GL in commercial databases on rural development, like AgECON CD and TROPAG CD, and conclusions drawn for presentation in the Fourth chapter.

3.21 References

Aina, L.O (1992) : Accession to development literature in Botswana. *Information Development,* 8(2), 104-108p.

______________ (93) : the problems of organising and disseminating of GL in Africa : Proceedings of the Ist International Conference on Grey Literature. Amsterdam : TransAtlantic, 169-174p.

Alberani Vilma, De Castro Pietrangeli Paola, Rossi Mazza Anna Maria (1990) : The use of Grey Literature in health sciences : A preliminary survey. *Bull.Med.Libr.Assoc,*78(4),358-363.

Auger, C.P (1998) : Information sources in Grey Literature. London : Bowker-Saur, 177p.

______________(1982) : Non-Conventional literature : Chairman's introduction. *Aslib proceedings,* 34 (11/12), Nov/Dec. 457-58p.

______________ (1994) : Grey Literature establishing a clear identity : Proceedings of the First International Conference on Grey Literature. 13-15,1993. Amsterdam : TransAtlantic, 1-4p.

Carroll, B.C and Cotter, G.A (1993) : A new generation of GL : the impact of advanced Information Technologies. 156p. In : Ist international conference on GL, Amsterdam : Transatlantic, 5-17p.

Encyclopedia of information and library science (1997) : edited by J. Feather and P Sturges .London : Routledge, 156p.

Kluck, Michael, M.A (1993) : The importance of Social Science Literature as a park of grey literature and the representation of social sciences in SIGLE. In. proceedings of the Ist international conference on GL, 13-15, Dec 93 . Amsterdam : transatlantic, 188p.

Lim, M.Y (1975) : AGRIS and the partier portion in it Southeast Asia, an Region, Msc. thesis

Mackenzie and Owen, J. S (1993) : Value and use of GL : The implications of networked publishing. Proceedings of the 3rd international conference on GL. Amsterdam : Transatlantic. 308-318p.

Owen, J.M (1997) : The expanding of horizon of GL. In . Proceedings of the 3rd international conference on GL. Amsterdam : Transatlantic.

Posnett & Reilly, P.M (1986) : Non-Conventional literature in tropical agricultural & National Agricultural Bibliography an assessment. *Quarterly Bull. of the international Association of Agricultural Libraries & Documentalists,* 31(1), 27-33p.

Posnett N.W and Baulkwill W.J (1982) : Working with Non-conventional Literature. *Journal of Information Science,* 5(4), 121-130p.

Rosa Di Cesare (1993). The impact evaluation of GL impact in physical sciences using bibliometric indicators preliminary results. In. Farace, D.J(ed) 1994, Proceedings of the Ist International Conference on GL. Amsterdam : Trans Atlantic publishing, 64-75p.

Howard, T.W (1993) : Electronic Distribution of Hypermedia on Wide-Area Networking Systems : An Update .*Technical Communication.* Third quarter, 438-448p.

Vickers, S and Wood, D.N (1982) : Improving the availability of Grey Literature. *Interlending Review.* 10(4), 125-130p.

Wilson (1964) : A communication perspective. Newbury park CA : Sage Publications.

Wood, D.N (1984) : Collection, Bibliographical Control, Access. *IFLA Journal*, 10(3), 278-283p.

4
Grey Literature and its Formats

4.1 Preprints

Preprints are research in progress reports to the small but often international group of fellow scientists working in the same relatively narrow research specialty. Like government research reports, the preprint is a primitive form of technical literature, not referred and unannounced but historical. Preprints are far more elusive than conference papers since only those on particular 'Preprint Circuits', know of their, existence even though they may be cited as references. To scientists on the research frontiers preprints are vital. The clue to their existence is in knowing who is doing what right now in relevant fields of research.

4.2 Report Literature

A technical report is an account of work done on a research project, which a scientist compiles to convey information to his employers or sponsors of the project and at the same time to other scientists working in the same or related field. The document may be, either a final report on a completed investigation or one of a series of reports which are issued at intervals to show how work is progressing on a particular investigation. The progress report is equally important compared to the final form because it includes negative results and incidental data which may be missing from a final report.

Present day research is undertaken not by individuals but by team of scientists working together in a laboratory of a Government research station, a university or an industrial organisation. The technical report is a more efficient method of recording the results of an investigation than the laboratory notebook, because it serves to disseminate results to anybody who receives a copy of the report. The most characteristic feature of report literature is the serial number given to each document. In American libraries the serial number often called the 'report series code'. The serial number is in fact usually a combination of letters and numbers which provides each report with a brief and unique identification e.g. ORNL-TM-4256 indicates Oak Ridge National Laboratory Technical Memorandum no. 4256.

A unique Problem of reports is Security classification. Reports are freely available are known as unclassified and those that are not 'classified'. Since there are commonly various grades of security classification - in order of ascending secrecy; restricted, confidential, secret and top secret as well as a 'declassified' category. The librarian finds in practice that even classified reports may be available if he show 'need to know'. And the librarian working with such reports may obliged to add to his burden by the need to control and even to 'log' their movements.

Reports are covered by most abstracting/indexing services and we find separate publications giving information about them. For example: Government Reports Announcements. Springfield, Virginia 1971 - Published by NTIS, covers reports, released to the public by US Government Departments and agencies. In India reports are covered to some extent by 'Indian Science Abstracts'. The Babha Atomic Research Centre Publishes. Bibliography of Current Reports' which includes reports and conference documents in the field of nuclear physics. 'ICSSR Newsletter" published by Indian Council of Social Science Research covers the reports published in social sciences.

4.3 Conference Proceedings

Papers presented at national and international conferences give a good indication of the present position of work in a subject field, especially with regard to the various, kinds of approach made by different workers. Some conferences are multi-disciplinary in character and proceedings of these bring together ideas from people in widely different subject are can stimulate new lines of enquiry. Proceedings may consist of papers (or a selection of them) Presented (or intended for presentation) at the conference, but can include the discussions in a condensed version or otherwise.

Conference proceedings may be published as a book, or as a part of a periodical, be mimeographed or exist only in manuscript form. They may appear a few weeks or a few years after the conference. They are either published by convening bodies, or by parent societies or by enterprising private publishers. Some times they are preprinted and not later published at all. At times they are made available only to those who attend the meetings or who write for them in time. Thus it is extremely difficult to identify and obtain. A conference variously known as a Colloquium, Congress, Convention, Seminar, Study Group, Summer School, Symposium, Work shop etc. sometimes preceded by 'International' or another term.

4.4 Patents

Patents are considered part of the primary-source literature, since an invention must be new in order to be patented and more often than, not there will be no other published description either of the idea or of its application. Patents are of particular interest to chemists and to engineers but the chemical are the only ones as a group that are well indexed, abstracted or listed by standard services. Announcement publications, abstracts journals and the individual patents are available from the various national patent offices and in selected depository libraries, but extensive searches require knowledge of both the subject, field and patent law.

4.5 Theses and Dissertations

Theses and dissertations (in practice the terms are interchangeable) give an account Of research done at a university or similar institution, generally as part of requirement for a Doctor's or Master's degree. Theses are intended to embody a certain amount of original work - indeed they often form the basis for one or more journal articles or monographs. If this work is later published in a journal it must be greatly condensed. In order to have the full view of the significant data the original source, has to be looked into.

4.6 Trade Literature or Manufacturers Literature

Those publications are often the, only source of specific information, about particular products on their development; if the information is not published elsewhere, this source becomes a primary source. Technical bulletins, data sheets, price lists and other specialised publications describing a manufacturers equipment or processes are, typical examples. The typical form of trade literature is a folder or pamphlet, glossily produced but commonly of an awkward non-standard size.

4.7 Statistical Sources

Statistical data is looked upon as an important source of information. It is used for analysis of problems and arriving at fruitful solutions, formulation of policies and plans and monitoring their progress. Much of it depends on the quality of data. Before using the data, however one should know the sources, process of collection, the reliability and the limitations. Unreliable and unauthoritative data may lead to faulty decisions and conclusions.

Statistics is collected, analyzed, organised and published by government bodies and autonomous institutions at national, state and district levels. International organisations also publish statistical data pertaining to global (different countries of the world). Statistical data occurs in all fields of knowledge but the well known and frequently used sources are: demographic data, industrial statistics, agricultural statistics, labour statistics, trade statistics, health statistics and financial statistics.

4.8 Survey reports

These reports are prepared for sponsored as well as non-sponsored projects.

4.9 Feasibility/detailed Project Report

These reports are prepared on request for industries who seek financial assistance through banks.

4.10 Literature note

This technical note is prepared for internal use before a project is taken up.

4.11 Process Know-how

A complete report is prepared when the project is sold to the interested party.

4.12 Basic Design

A report is prepared on request for the machinery and equipment required for the processor.

4.13 Detailed Design report

This document covers the mechanical aspects also.

4.14 Demonstration report

This report is confidential and is signed and sealed by the Laboratory and the industrial entrepreneur.

4.15 Operation and shutdown manuals

These manuals give details of operation and shut down of a person.

4.16 Government Documents

That the proliferating organs/agencies of the Union and State governments produce the single largest group of documents in the field of socioeconomic development needs no emphasis. In a sense, the entire range of these documents may be labeled as "grey" literature. Only a small percentage, which in the judgment of the sponsoring agencies qualify for wider dissemination, is distributed through commercial channels, but the legendary inefficiency of the distribution system makes even these documents virtually inaccessible.

While all organs of the four branches (executive, judiciary, parliamentary and legislative, and constitutional) of the government are the potential sources of "grey" literature, we shall focus on two in the executive branch which generate documents of considerable socioeconomic significance, primarily for internal use: (a) research oriented agencies, and (b) Committees and Commissions. Most of the documents of other agencies are by-products of administrative activities, and their process of generation is known. Similarly, the functions of the three branches are rather well defined, since they are governed by statutory and constitutional provisions. The publications brought out by them are also administrative by-products. Access to their documents may be difficult but not formidable. This, however, is not to suggest their exclusion from a "grey" literature information system.

The research oriented agencies have more than one function: administrative, regulatory, advisory, and policy-making. While in some cases, the nature of their activities is of research type, some agencies undertake studies and research primarily to support the four functions. The agencies may be grouped into four categories:

(a) Agencies involved in socioeconomic planning, e. g., Planning Commission, State Departments/Boards of Planning.

(b) Agencies for data collection, processing, dissemination, and maintenance at the Union and State levels, e. g., Office of the Registrar General, Central Statistical Organisation, State Statistical Bureaus.

(c) Advisory bodies and research wings attached to economic ministries/departments and regulatory agencies, e. g., Office of the Economic Advisers, Ministries of Commerce and Industries, Agricultural Prices Commission, Department of Economic Analysis and Policy (Reserve Bank of India), Bureau of Industrial Costs and Prices, Transport Research Division (Ministry of Shipping & Transport).

(d) Agencies established to undertake survey, exploration, and conservation of natural resources, e. g., Geological Survey Of India, Central Ground Water Board, National Remote Sensing Agency.

A substantial number of documents originating in these organisations are of the "grey" variety. For example, the enormous planning exercise undertaken by the Union and State planning machineries generate a plethora of documents not generally known outside the Organisations .

Besides the reports of the working groups and the project reports, the documents prepared by the Planning Commission include: plan approach documents, preparatory documents like working and position papers, and reports of sponsored, research, reports of parliamentary committees to consider the draft plans, papers relating to the meetings of the National Development Council, guidelines for the formulation of State plans, report's of appraisal and evaluation of plan programmes and projects.

The reports of the Committees and Commissions (including those variously designated as Working Group, Study Group, Task Force, Steering Committee) are extremely important source of information for three reasons: (a) they present comprehensive background information about the problems being studied; (b) they generally contain facts and data not available elsewhere, since the Committees/ Commissions have access to internal sources of information; and (c). they are indicative of policy decisions of the Government. Some Commissions dealing with issues having wider implications (e. g., National Commission of Labour, National Commission of Agriculture, National Police Commission), constitute study groups and sponsor studies to examine specific problems. A perusal of the annual reports of the various administrative departments (e.g. Annual Report of the Planning Commission mentioned earlier) as well as of the regulatory agencies (e. g., Annual Report and the Report on Currency and Finance, Reserve Bank of India) would give some idea about the number of Committees that are set up every year. Only the reports of a small number of committees that are considered of wider public interest are released through the commercial channels. Generally speaking, the important of the reports is under appreciated by the majority of researchers.

4.17 Project Feasibility Reports

Preparation of full-scale feasibility reports (now an "industry" by itself) is almost mandatory for a project (social, infrastructural, or industrial) to become a candidate for investment funds or for inclusion in development plans. Such reports, generally prepared by the consultancy and research organisations, contain valuable data gathered from various primary and secondary sources. After the reports are put to a limited rise for the appraisal of projects, this wealth of data remains buried in the archives of the financial institutions, the Planning Commission, and government departments.

4.18 Working Papers

As has been mentioned earlier, working papers are interim publications and may be considered as drafts of potential journal articles, although the vast majority may never be formally published at all. They are commonly type script, mimeographed, and issued in a numbered series (e. g., Working Papers, World Employment Programme Research, International Labour Office) by the author's employing institutions. They often bear a caveat that the draft is preliminary and intended for discussion (and hence also labeled as "Discussion Papers" series), and therefore should not be quoted. The reasons for the proliferation of working papers are:

(a) to overcome the delay involved in formal publications.

(b) to establish priority of innovation over others working in the same area, and to protect against plagiarism.

(c) to benefit from the comments of colleagues and peers

before the authors re-work them for eventual publication in journals.

But more importantly, the urge to gain visibility prompts the researchers and their institutions to adopt this interim dissemination measure. Many are also painfully aware of the increasing competition in getting entry into the formal dissemination channels.

4.19 Research Reports

Many working papers report results of research and in that sense they may be called "research reports". While working papers, by design and intent, are interim dissemination measures, the research reports considered here, on the other hand, are the final outputs of research activities; and in this final form they are submitted to the funding agencies. However, as has been mentioned earlier, both the research reports and working papers are interim publications. The report literature has been growing steadily in size and importance in development studies in recent years. Several national science agencies like the Indian Council of Social Science Research, the Council of Scientific and Industrial Research and ministries and departments like the Home, Planning Commission (which had revived its research funding programme), Environment, Energy, provide research funds to academic and research institutions. Only a small number of reports thus generated ultimately culminate in formal publications. Not many publishers are inclined, for economic reasons, to publish books based on the reports. Most research grants do not have any provision for dissemination of results since the inseparability of research and dissemination activities is not fully appreciated

4.20 Seminar Papers

Bibliographical control of the documents the local, relating to the ever increasing number of seminars at the local, national, and international levels continues to baffle the information men. Advance information about the international conferences is generally available (national conferences in a lesser degree), but seminars organised by different institutions and organisations remain largely unknown to many. While commercial sources represent the single largest group in terms of the number of seminar proceedings published or distributed, they represent the smallest single element, compared to the total output of seminar-related literature. Seminar papers are generally made available to participants before they are formally presented at the seminars (hence also called "preprints") by their authors.

The practice regarding the publication of seminar papers, after the meetings take place, varies. In ideal cases, the papers are reviewed, and only the selected ones are published along with the records of discussion. Other papers are either merely listed or only their abstracts are incorporated in the publication. There are also many instances of publishing unedited and unreferred seminar papers using photo-offset method with or without the records of discussion. Many seminar papers are never published.

The main criticism of seminar papers is that, since in many cases seminars are unplanned, papers are not properly screened, and that authors write under pressure at the cost of quality.

4.21 Standards

According to American National Standards Institution, a standard is a specification accepted by recognized authority as the most practical and appropriate current solution of a recurring problem. A specification is a concise statement of the required standard for a material, process, method, procedure or service. Standards may be interpreted as a pattern of an ideal, a model procedure, a measure for an appraisal, a stimulus for future development and improvement and, an instrument to assist decision. The specifications help to know the procedures widely followed. It is also a social responsibility of the country to safeguard the people against the hazards that are likely to be caused while operating the machinery. The governments by putting their mark or standardization on a product are ensuring the safety of the product Clientele of special libraries are in need of information about the product quality and reliability. This can be known properly when the product conforms to particular specifications. The specifications achieve universal standardization of products so that the consistency in their performance is maintained. The importance of standards collection in a special library hardly needs emphasis. Standards and specifications are formulated by companies, trade associations, professional bodies, government agencies, national standardising organisations, and international standards agencies.

4.22 Annual Reports

Annual Reports gives the details about the institution and its various activities of the particular year. And also helps to get a broad idea about the subjects or topics in which the institutions are likely to be interested. A list of projects randomly selected from the Annual Reports of several institutions will indicate the types of projects sponsored by different agencies.

5
Use Pattern of Grey Literature by Social Scientists

5.1 Introduction

"User studies" to determine the pattern of usage of literature in a given subject area, based on scientific lines, are an accepted means of research in library science. The methodologies adopted in determining the use pattern vary. Apart from administering a questionnaire to individual users, citation analysis is one another accepted method not only to determine the kind of literature used but also ranking the most used sources such as journals.

In this chapter, the researcher used both the above methods to highlight the importance shown by the users to GL. Firstly using citation analysis, the articles published in the Journal of Rural Development (JRD) for 16 years from 1982-97, were analysed to identify the distribution of GL, subjects covered and how JRD fared in comparison with international sources. Simultaneously, various questions administered through a questionnaire were also analysed to determine the use pattern of GL in their various dimensions.

5.2 Use pattern of GL Based on Citation Analysis

The researcher made an attempt to study the use pattern of GL by taking a representative journal in the field of rural development in India, using citation analysis. Journal of Rural Development (JRD) is an official journal of the National Institute of Rural Development. It carries both theoretical and empirical research based articles pertaining to India and other developing countries. Besides, it publishes case studies, research notes, and book reviews. The journal aims at promoting study and research in rural development. It provides a forum for exchange of views between various social science disciplines and the policy makers, planners and the executives concerned with rural development. For the purpose of the present in depth study the JRD is examined for sixteen years covering the period from 1982-1997. (T.Ramadevi, 1999).

As the aim of the study is to understand the use pattern of grey literature by the social scientists with special reference to the faculty of NIRD, the data relating to the type of articles that are published in the journal are examined regarding their number, focus, the number of citations, the category of citations and their distribution together with other details.

As the citation analysis is one of the accepted methods to assess or determine the actual use pattern of documents and resources, for scientific communication this method was chosen to investigate the use of GL. Analysis of such citation can reveal useful information like the relative use of different categories of documents such as conferences, seminars,workshop proceedings, research reports, committee and commission reports, annual reports etc. Additionally the data that was derived from JRD pertaining to GL was compared with that of the two international abstracting services like Rural Development Abstracts(AgECON) of CABI, U.K and Abstracts of Tropical Agriculture (TROPAG) brought out by the Royal Tropical Institute, Netherlands. While comparing the two international abstracting journals, the coverage of GL for the period 1982-97 pertaining to India was taken into consideration. This was done in order to know the extent of coverage as well as the categorisation of materials to compare and match with the data obtained from the JRD and also to understand the kind of accessibility and availability of GL for the purposes of citation as well as for bibliographic control. The coverage of GL for the period 1982-97 was seen by using the database available under the name AgECON CD and

TROPAG CD respectively. The CD search was restricted to the GL on India without any restrictions on place of publication. It is observed that these international abstracting services are able to cover most of the conference/seminar proceedings, and case studies etc., The study reveals that the increasing number of citations of grey literature references indicate the increased importance and use of GL.

5.2.1 Distribution of Citations : The following table 2 shows the total number of references and total number of grey references among the cited with five year breakup .

Table 2 Distribution of citations and percentage of grey references

	1982-86	1987-91	1992-97	Total
Total no. of cited references in JRD	572	2292	1903	4767
Total no. of grey references among the cited	148	597	581	1326
Percentage	25.8%	26%	30.5%	27.8%

The above table shows distribution of articles in a five year interval along with the number of citations and the percentage of grey literature references among the cited. It is interesting to know that there is an increasing trend in the citation of grey literature progressively over the years. This can be attributed to two factors (1) the increasing production of grey literature (2) and its relative awareness and accessibility.

5.2.2 Subject coverage of GL : The researcher has also analysed the kind of subjects the cited grey literature cover as well as their type. The following table 3 gives the various subjects covered in the articles contributed to JRD as well as the corresponding percentage of citation belonging to that topic of the contribution.

Table 3. Subject Coverage of Grey Literature in JRD

Subject of Articles		*Subject of Citations given in the articles*	
Rural Development	116(19.4%)	Rural Development	231(17.4%)
Agriculture	90(15%)	Agriculture	135(10.1%)
Local Government / Panchayati Raj	65(10.9%)	Local Government	147(11%)
Gender	38(6.3%)	Gender	55(4.1%)
Industry	31(5.2%)	Industry	40(3.0%)
Forestry	4(0.6%)	Forestry	43(3.2%)
Poverty	30(5.0%)	Poverty	40(3.0%)
Total	596	Total	1326

Note : Remaining subjects like energy, employment, livestock, watershed, finances and many others which have cited twice or once are not given here.

JRD by virtue of its stated focus, attracted articles more in number that relate to rural development followed by allied subjects like agriculture, local government, and gender studies. Very interestingly citations also follow more or less the same pattern.

5.2.3 Grey Literature in Different Databases : In order to understand the kind of accessibility and availability of grey literature for the purposes of citation as well as bibliographic control, two major international abstracting services AgECON and TROPAG were examined. The coverage of grey literature for the period 1982-97 was seen by using the databases available under the name AgECON CD and TROPAG CD respectively. The CD search was restricted to the grey literature on India without any restrictions on place of publication. The table 4 gives the distribution of grey literature citations as against the total references in case of the JRD and total entries in case of two CDs pertaining to India.

Table 4. Grey literature in different databases

Total references for the period	*JRD*	*AgECONCD*	*TROPAG*
1982-1997	4767	21887	14329
Grey references	1326 (28%)	3803 (17.3%)	1241 (8.6%)

We are comparing here grey references in JRD a primary journal, with that of the grey references abstracted pertaining to India in two secondary periodical databases for the same period of 1982-97. The use of GL to some extent is influenced by its coverage in the secondary periodicals. If the number of refernces of GL in secondary periodicals increases, then simultaneously its effects on the citation in the primary periodicals. With this in view the researcher made an attempt to compare these two kinds of periodicals, primary and secondary.

However, it is also observed that the international abstracting services are able to cover most of the conference/ seminar proceedings, case studies, dissertations etc. It may solve the problem of poor bibliographical control to some extent. It can be concluded from the above analysis that grey literature in various forms, even in the present day context, continues to be one of the important media of transfer of information and a source of recorded knowledge but eludes comprehensive bibliographical control. Increasing number of citations of grey literature references indicates the increased importance and use of grey literature.

5.3 Use Pattern of GL : Analysis of data derived from questionnaires

Social Scientists are involved in programmes such as training, conducting research on various social problems, where they use GL for different purposes besides teaching in universities and institutions of higher learning. Here an attempt has been made to study how the awareness of GL is created to access and make it available together with the problems faced and suggestions made by the users for its smooth flow. Importance of grey literature as a source of information for social scientists is established through review of literature. However, as stated in our first chapter the use pattern by social scientists was not brought out clearly in any of the studies undertaken so far. As a result, the awareness, accessibility and use of grey literature by social scientists is itself a matter for assessment which is attempted by the researcher through a questionnaire designed for the purpose.

For the purpose of the study the researcher distributed 200 questionnaires in 9 organisations, out of which 3 are universities and 6 are Research and Training institutions in Hyderabad. Out of 200 questionnaires administered 150 (75%) filled in questionnaires were received.

The sample consists of social scientists holding positions such as Professors, Directors, Research Officers, Research Associates, Research Scholars. Structured questionnaires were distributed to elicit the qualitative and quantitative data such as qualifications of respondents, nature of work, areas of specialization, experience in research, knowledge about GL, use of various information sources, development of personal collection, attendance to seminars, familiarity with internet etc. The data collected through the questionnaires tabulated and SPSS is used for its analysis. The analysis and inferences are discussed in the following paragraphs.

5.3.1 Age group : The scholars research work and use of literature depends on several factors. Age is one of such factors that influences the quality of research work. Naturally as the age of the scholar increases, the following effects are possible. a) the person is likely to be senior in the field b) Develops increased awareness of the subject. c) Develops maturity d) Possibility of associating with more number of research/ projects . With age exposure increases, and so also the experience in the field of specialisation. It plays an important role in creating awareness level and use of literature especially GL. The table 5 indicates the respondents age

Table 5. Age group of the respondents

	1	*2*	*3*	*4*	*Total*
Age	(21-30)	(31-40)	(41-50)	(50+)	
No. of Respondents	23(15.3%)	32(21.3%)	63(42%)	32(21.3%)	150

The majority of the respondents 63(42%) fall under the age group of 41-50 followed by 32(21.3%) under the age group of 50+. A total of 95 (63.3%) respondents are between the age group of 40-60 which is considered to be mature, fairly senior in the hierarchy. Therefore, the sample represents potential/ actual users of GL for a long period. The data collected from the sample is found to be relevant for the study and may help to assess the use of GL by the social scientists.

5.3.2 Gender : The subject social science deals with the people and society .The approach and attitudes of the people vary from individual to individual based on their cultural background, economic conditions etc. The gender also influences the social structure and society. The table 6 shows gender representation.

Table 6. Gender representation

Gender	*No.*	*Percentage*
Male	133	88.7%
Female	17	11.3%

The representation of female in the sample is less compared to male. This situation can perhaps be expected as it represents the general trend in the Indian society. However, an attempt is made here to give more weightage to their responses, as they are found to be very active researchers.

5.3 .3 Qualifications : Generally the research activities are initiated during or after post graduate education and when the social scientists settle in their profession. At that time they are likely to be familiar with various types of information sources including GL. Therefore the qualifications may have a bearing on the use of GL. The following table 7 shows the qualifications of the respondents.

Table 7. Qualifications of the Respondents

1	2	3	4	
M.A.	**Mphil**	**PhD**	**PG/Diploma**	**Total**
8(5.3)	39(26)	99(66)	4(2.7)	150

Qualifications of the respondents are grouped into 4 categories as shown in the table 7. The third group with Ph.D, is the largest group with 99 (66%) followed by 2nd group respondents with Mphil are39(26%). The data shows that a total of 92% of respondents have good research experience as they have completed their Mphil and Ph.D. It infers that the sample taken for the study consists of highly qualified persons who are knowledgeable about GL. Hence the sample taken for the study is appropriate.

5.3.4 Type of institution : The organisations in Hyderabad, involved in social science research, training and academic activity are identified. These institutions are producing a lot of GL as a part of their own activities. Therefore the activities of the institutions shall have an influence on its faculty. Necessary care had been taken to identify and select the institutions for research and they had been categorised into Research and Training Institutions and Universities. The following table 8 shows the respondents from the two categories.

Table 8. Number of respondents from different institutions.

Research and Training Institutions	95 (63.3)
Universities	55 (36.7)
	Total 150

Out of 150 respondents, 63.5% of respondents are primarily engaged in research and training, remaining 36.7% are fully engaged in teaching. The respondents were engaged in various activities and they seemed to have been exposed to different kinds of literature at different stages of their careers. Therefore the sample chosen for the study is likely to be relevant.

5.3.5 Area of Specialisation : Social science is inter-disciplinary in nature, and as stated earlier deals with the problems of the society. To understand the social environment of an individual there is a need to study the society from different angles. Therefore the researcher felt the need to pick up the respondents having different subject backgrounds. The area of specialization was left to the respondents to identify. The subjects/area of specialisation of the respondents chosen for the study is given in table 9 .

It can be seen that many respondents are having specialisation in more than one subject. These include interdisciplinary areas like Rural Development, local government, project planning, participatory rural appraisal, agricultural extension, weaker sections etc.

It can be inferred from the above that many areas are covered where the output of GL is maximum in the social sciences as a whole, though it may vary from discipline to discipline. The researcher attempted to touch all the areas of social sciences. As a result the conclusions drawn after the survey would appear to be more valid.

5.3.6 Information Sources of GL : As information is growing enormously, it is very difficult to trace out the required piece of information. It is available in different formats and the researcher has to put more efforts to access particularly the GL. There are two types of information sources one is informal another is formal. The informal sources are like friends, meetings, chat groups. The researcher may have the informal network (invisible college) in his own field of specialisation. In this network, scholars have a periodic meetings to discuss on various issues of their specilaisation. During conferences normally the participants discuss various aspects of their subjects of interest. Chat groups/Institutional meetings are also the best sources of information. The researcher made an attempt to know how best the available information sources are useful to the respondents and how much importance they are giving to the sources.

There are formal sources like Newsletters which give the information about the activities of the association / organisation. TV/Radio, Newspapers and Magazines are also important information sources under mass media. Some of the other sources like libraries help the researcher to trace the document and enable them to use in right time. Information sources preferred by social scientists were given in table 10.

Table 9. Area of Specialisation

Subjects	*No. of respondents*
Economics	28
Rural Development	20
Management	18
Local Government	15
Man and Environment	12
Finance	9
Politics and Pubic administration	8
Project planning	7
History	7
Agricultural extension	5
Marketing	5
Women Studies	5
Participatory Rural Appraisal	5
Information Technology	4
Human resource	4
Training Methods	4
Employment	3
Anthropology	3

Table 10. Information sources Informal sources

Rank	*00*	*01*	*02*	*03*	*04*	*05*	*06*	*07*	*08*	*09*
Friends	24	39	31	18	13	15	3	3	3	1
Conferences	21	36	35	29	13	11	2	1	2	0
Chat Groups	51	8	22	13	19	8	11	9	8	1
Instt./Internal Meetings	41	23	14	30	23	7	9	3	0	0
Internet	52	8	7	16	17	28	9	4	2	7

Formal sources

Rank	*00*	*01*	*02*	*03*	*04*	*05*	*06*	*07*	*08*	*09*
Newsletters	66	25	12	12	18	11	3	0	0	1
Mass Media	89	5	7	15	10	16	5	1	1	1
Libraries	6	86	34	10	11	21	1	0	0	0
Newspapers	39	17	28	22	11	14	8	8	2	1
Magazines	86	5	13	9	19	13	4	0	0	1
Others	130	5	2	0	2	1	7	0	0	3

The respondents identified the information sources and gave rank on the basis of their use. Majority of the respondents 86 (57.3%) significantly chose the library as the number one source for information in social sciences in general. They gave top priority to the in-house resources compared to other sources. 34 (22.6%) respondents had given second preference to the library, 10 respondents preferred library as a third important information source. A total of 130 (86.6%) respondents gave either first or second or third priority for the library. This is also interesting to note that the respondents would prefer to use the internal resources like library first before they go to tap other sources like friends, conference proceedings and print materials. As noted earlier, due to the very nature of GL, it would be difficult to track the existence of GL individually. The respondents felt that an institution like library is found to be the first major source of information to access the GL.

The second preference in the first priority is given by the respondents for friends and peer groups. These people are likely to have similar interests being colleagues in the work place which is congenial for exchange of ideas. They constantly interact with each other for exchange of knowledge and to find solutions to problems.

The conferences occupy the third position. Normally the participants of a seminar present the papers based on the latest studies conducted in their own field. Social scientists prefer to participate in the conferences/workshops and seminars to keep themselves abreast with the latest developments in their area.

In the second priority conferences occupy the first rank with 35(23.3%) respondents, followed by libraries with 34(22.6%) respondents, and 31(20.6%) respondents gave third preference to friends.

The sources assigned with the print and other media like news papers, magazines, newsletters, mass media did not attract high rank. Internet as an information source, interestingly, does not attract the kind of priority expected,. though the internet presence is very much felt. Based on the observation the researcher felt that most of the institutions are not equipped fully with internet may be due to problems in infrastructure,, connectivity, lack of training in its use or bandwidth problems. This might have dampened the interest of the respondents in making it as a major source of information. There is a need to equip the institutions with internet and give more orientation to the researchers in surfing the internet to find out the latest research trends and findings.

Awareness score was derived using the following formula

$$\text{Awareness score} = \left\{ \sum_{i=1}^{5} \text{ifi} / 5 \times \Sigma\, \text{fi} \right\} \times 100$$

Where fi stands foı the frequency of responses against source (i = 1,2,3,4.5.)

It is weighted average measure. The awareness scores are respectively, 76.5 for informal sources and 63.7 for formal sources . Awareness score varies from 20 to 100 on a five point scale, the lowest value will be 1 and the highest value will be 5. The former indicates a very low level of awareness while the latter points out full awareness. The average score of 76.5 for informal sources and 63.7 for formal sources indicate that respondents were more familiar with the informal sources than the formal sources. Further, the awareness levels were high suggesting that the respondents are knowledgeable persons.

5.3.7 Purpose and use of GL : Social scientists are using different types of material including GL to support the research and training activities. They stated that the grey literature is being used for the following purposes.

* GL is being used to know about the latest developments in their field of interest.
* GL is used at the time of selecting a research problem.
* To update the knowledge in the area of specialisation.

The above qualitative data indicates that the GL is one of the most useful information sources for the research and academic activities. It plays a vital role on par with other information sources. As GL is likely to be extensively used, the libraries have to put special efforts to procure and organize the GL collection. It can also be concluded that the library alone is likely to play an important role in information retrieval. The librarians need to keep track of publications of GL to provide nascent micro literature to the users.

5.3.8 Personal Collection Development : Every researcher maintains the personal collection for reference as well as for updating their subject knowledge. The acquisition of information resources is a continuous process. The type of materials procured vary from researcher to researcher. The materials include books, journals and other print materials such as reports, training materials, thesis etc. The researcher looks for the content of the document and try to procure the relevant material for his personal collection. Further, he/she may meet several other fellow researchers, attend the conferences/meetings and visit the libraries, wherein he/she finds the useful material and wishes to the same to their personal collection. The personal collection is repeatedly used for academic or research activities.

Every researcher tries to buildup his personal collection by using various methods. The personal collection includes materials such as pamphlets, brochures, training materials, reprints, research reports and conference proceedings. As members of peer groups, the social scientists also circulate the preprints and reports among themselves for review and recognition. This personal collection is very valuable reference source and it contains mostly the GL literature, as seen from table 11.

Based on the data received, the personal collection is classified into five groups, with increasing number of publications in each group. A majority of the respondents are having the personal collection up to 5 publications. Within the collection of 5 publications 105 (70) respondents having the conference reports, 104 (69) have the theses collection, 80(53.3) having occasional papers 84(56) are having the statistical data, 83 (55.3) are having the collection of annual reports, 71 (47.3) are having pre/reprints, 45 (30) are having research reports etc.

Table 11. Collection development of GL by the respondents

Title of collections	*No. of Collections*					
	Nil	*(1-5)*	*(6-10)*	*(11-15)*	*(16-20)*	*(20+)*
Research Reports	18	45	38	25	14	10
Conference Proceedings	26	105	15	04	00	00
Occasional Papers	48	80	10	02	03	07
Thesis	35	104	06	02	01	02
Preprints/Reprints	35	71	26	03	06	09
Training Materials	95	34	13	03	02	03
Statistical Data	47	84	08	06	02	03
Personal Correspondence	90	45	08	04	02	01
Annual Reports	48	83	12	00	02	05
Others	103	17	10	14	02	04

The data also shows that many of the respondents are having a good personal collection of conference proceedings, thesis, statistical data, annual reports, occasional papers followed by research reports. Study may also infer that the social scientists prefer collection of GL documents which are closely related to their area of specialization.

Table 12. Personal Collection of GL - Average and model value.

GL Items	*Over all Average*	*No of respondents possessing GL (Personal Collection) Items*			
		0	*1-5*	*5-10*	*10 & Above*
Research Reports	10.08 (11.37)	17	49*	36	48
Preprints/Reprints	5.86 (7.64)	25	107*	14	4
Statistical Data	3.09 (4.64)	48	79*	12	11
Conference Proceedings	3.01 (3.62)	35	103*	5	7
Occasional Papers	4.54 (6.68)	35	75*	23	17
Thesis/Dissertations	2.29 (2.98)	98	32*	12	8
Training material	2.36 (6.81)	50	83*	8	9
Personal correspondence	1.45 (3.76)	92	44*	9	5
Annual reports	2.53 (3.72)	48	86*	10	6

*Represents the model category. I.e. "1-5" for all the GL items.

N.B : Figures in parentheses are average number of collections excluding the persons with no personal collection.

Most of the respondents were having GL personal collection in the range of "1-5" (modal value). However, in the case of Research Reports, many of the respondents possessed

GL types more than 10. Based on the average number of items/ collections regarding various types of material the following appear to be more popular . Research Reports, Preprints/ Reprints, Occasional papers, Statistical Data, Conference proceedings etc. as seen in table 12, Figs 3 and 4.

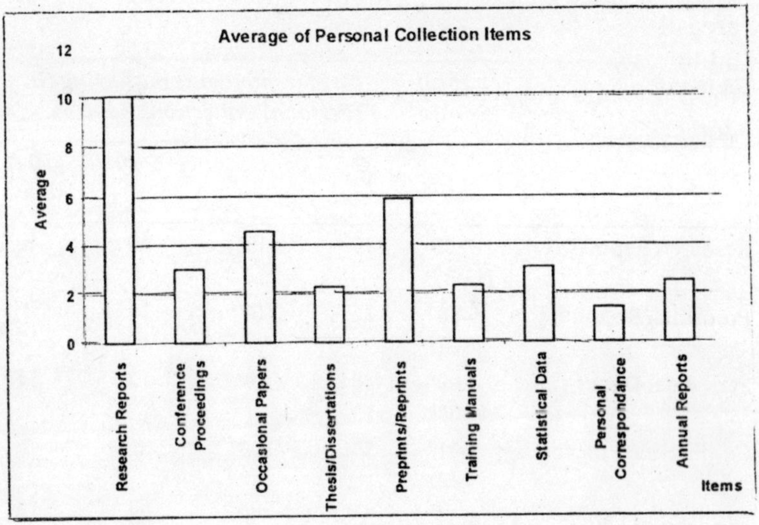

Fig. 4

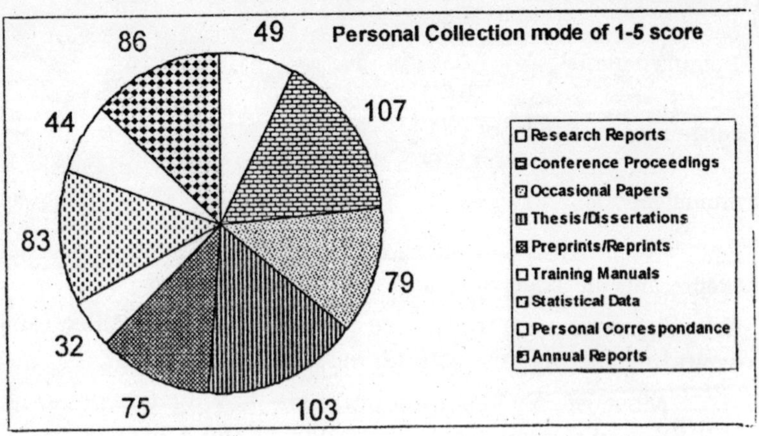

Fig. 5

5.3.9 Secondary sources : Secondary sources like abstracting and indexing services are used for identification and awareness creation about the primary documents. They give the complete bibliographical details. Social scientists do refer the secondary journals to get awareness of the new articles, books, reports and other material which are published in their area of specialization. Many of the sources also cover the GL in addition to the periodical literature . In the process of identifying the published articles, the researcher get to know about the GL, and consequently the use of GL. The following table 13 shows the use of secondary sources.

Table 13. Use of secondary sources

Yes	*No*	*Total*
120(80%)	31(20%)	150

Out of 150 respondents 120(80%) are using secondary sources for their information needs. Further they have stated that the secondary journals cover information regarding various types of GL such as research reports, conference proceedings, occasional papers etc. published by different organizations. They also stated that the coverage of GL is relatively less compared to periodical literature.

They also felt that if GL is covered comprehensively in the secondary sources, the demand for GL may increase enormously and it becomes as an important information source for the scholars.

5.3.10 Membership in professional Associations : Membership in professional associations make the social scientists feel that they belong to a professional community. Therefore most of the social scientists join as a member in one or more professional associations in order to be in the mainstream and to know what type of research problems the peer groups are working with.. This will also provide an opportunity to exchange ideas. Further, membership helps in knowing the latest developments that are taking place around them in their area of specialization. The following table 14 shows the membership of the respondents in the associations.

Table 14 Membership in professional Associations

Yes	*No*	*Total*
104(69.3%)	46(31%)	150

The respondents also stated that the Association's publications may help to get aware and also keep track of the grey publications published by these associations. The newsletters of the Association may help to know where the information is getting generated, when it is published and whom to contact, etc.

The above analysis shows that the social scientists are becoming more and more involved in professional associations and the generators of GL may prefer the Association publications to publicise their products, so that GL will reach many of the social scientists. The products of the professional associations like newsletters, bulletins are found to be useful to make the professionals alert and abreast of the latest developments. The Association publications can be used as a platform by the researchers to disseminate their products to the wider audience.

5.3.11 Attendance in Seminars/Conferences/ Workshops : Conferences/Seminars will bring the scholars of similar subject interest to one platform. They provide an occasion to bring together old and new fellow scholars for exchange of ideas. The conferences enhance the awareness level about the scholars who are working in their area. This may lead to the development of continuous interaction with the scholars. It also enable them to acquire conference proceedings and other materials/brochures, newsletters. Most of this type of literature as seen, may likely to add into the personal collection. Therefore the social scientists prefer to attend one or more conferences in an year. The following table 15 shows the attendance to conferences/seminars.

Table 15. Attendance in seminars

No of Seminars Attended	*One*	*Two*	*Two+*	*Total*
Respondents	64 (42.7 %)	38(25.3%)	48(32 %)	150

The data shows that 64 (42.7%) attended at least one conference in an year. 38 (25.3%) have attended two conferences in an year. Therefore, 102 (68%) respondents are attending conferences one or two. On the basis of interaction it has been found that the respondents would try to procure the conference proceedings which are relevant to their working even if they could not personally attend the same.

5.3.12 Acquisition of GL Material : Any library's main duty is to procure and disseminate information about relevant documents which satisfy the information needs of the users. It attempts to collect variety of documents. GL is one such variety. Out of 150 respondents 143(95.3) respondents replied that their library is procuring annual reports, government publications, research reports etc., which are all part of GL.

The data indicates that almost all the libraries are procuring GL. The respondents mentioned in the table 10, that their library ranked as first or second most important information source for the users. This may be due to the reason that they are procuring the macro and micro literature which provides satisfaction to the users. Further it may also be concluded that the libraries have recognized the importance of GL for their users. The accessing of GL is likely to be increased if this trend continues .

5.3.13 Priority use of GL material : GL being used by different scholars for different purposes. The researchers are interested in getting the research reports, the trainer may prefer to have latest training modules, the statistician would prefer the statistical data to know the trend. In this study an attempt has been made to assess the priority in using various types of GL documents. The following table 16 indicates the priority wise ranking of the GL documents

Table 16. Priority wise use of GL

GL items	*Ranking*									
	0	*01*	*02*	*03*	*04*	*05*	*06*	*07*	*08*	*09*
Research Reports	8	59	38	21	12	5	2	4	0	1
	(5.3)	(39.3)	(25.3)	(14)	(8)	(3.3)	(1.3)	(2.7)		(0.7)
Conferences	14	12	23	25	30	18	16	1	0	
	(9.3)	(8)	(15.3)	(16.7)	(20)	(7.3)	(10.7)	(0.7)		
Occasional Paper	17	13	18	25	25	21	19	9	3	0
	(11.3)	(8.7)	(12)	(16.7)	(16.7)	(14)	(12.7)	(6)	(2)	
Thesis	33	7	10	20	0	15	20	14	6	5
	(22)	(4.7)	(6.7)	(13.3)		(10)	(13.3)	(9.3)	(10.7)	(3.3)
Pre/reprints	36	8	11	15	21	16	12	11	20	0
	(24)	(5.3)	(7.3)	(10)	(14)	(10.7)	(8)	(7.3)	(13.3)	
Training Material	44	12	9	9	16	14	20	15	8	3
	(29.3)	(8)	(6)	(6)	(10.7)	(9.3)	(13.3)	(10)	(5.3)	(2)
Statistical Data	18	28	16	20	12	14	22	17	2	1
	(12)	(18.7)	(10.7)	(13.3)	(8)	(9.3)	(14.7)	(11.3)	(1.3)	(0.7)
Annual Reports	25	16	21	8	14	21	12	15	14	4
	(16.7)	(10.7)	(14)	(5.3)	(9.3)	(14)	(8)	(10)	(9.3)	(2.7)
Others	117	6	2	5	0	5	2	0	3	10
	(78)	(4)	(1.3)	(3.2)		(3.3)	(1.3)		(2.0)	(6.7)

A total of 59(39.3%) respondents ranked research reports as the first priority followed by statistical data 28(18.7), annual reports 16 (10.7) occasional papers 13(8.7) training materials 12 (8) etc. More or less the same trend is seen in the second priority also.

The respondents gave top priority to the research reports may be due to the very nature of the nascent information contained in it. Statistical data helps the researcher to substantiate his arguments and draw valid conclusions. The importance is indicated by putting it as a second priority. Varied types of GL is being used by researchers with varied priority. Therefore it can be concluded that every type of GL material is useful for research/training and academic activities. The libraries have to make note of this and procure from time to time and add them into the collection. Fortunately the respondents considered that the library is an important information source to access GL and they also have considerable collection of GL material in their personal collection.

5.3.14 mn Rankings : To test the hypothesis i.e. whether there is significant difference in the perceptions of the respondents with reference to GL documents . The mn ranking method was employed. This method helps in determining the degree of consistancy among the respondents with reference to their preference of different GL item (i.e. their usefulness). This method is used when respondents (m) rank order the subjects (n) based on certain criteria. Consistency in the ranking of subjects can be verified through this mn ranking method. The statistical measure adopted is 'w', coefficient of concordance which lies between 0 and 1. A value close to '1' indicates consistency among judgements and the average ranking can be accepted as a representative one. That is, the above contention is in broad agreement among the respondents. On the contrary a low value of 'w' and close to zero implies that respondents significantly differ in ranking the subjects and the average ranking cannot be acceptable as a common pattern. So, whenever 'w' value is low, the hypothesis is rejected and significant variations in the perceptions are confirmed.

Inference : From the value of w and above analyses, it can be concluded that the respondents assign broadly the similar importance to the various GL formats. The average ranking can be taken as broad view of the perceptions of social science community. Thus among the GL formats the most important are research reports, preprints and occasional papers.

5.3.15 Information Services provided by the Libraries : The libraries are using different techniques and offer services to create awareness about new arrivals. They are like current awareness services, alert services, accession lists etc. Such services fulfill the five laws of library science .Similar services should be organised for GL also to increase the level of awareness and to enhance its usage. It may be noted that the nature of GL is different from other literature which needs special attention in disseminating the GL. On the basis of data, it is noted the following practices are adopted by different libraries to disseminate the information.

* Some libraries are informing to their users about the new arrivals through notes
* Some are informing through Bulletins.
* Some libraries are informing at the library counter.
* Libraries are informing by using email services and through LAN
* A few libraries are maintaining registers for this purpose.

However,there is no uniformity in practice. A standard or uniform procedure needs to be practiced to enhance the use of GL .The libraries should take advantage of IT and use it as a tool to communicate the availability of GL among the libraries . They should plan to introduce services using email to increase the level of awareness and accessibility.

5.3.16 Availability of GL in the Library : Most of the respondents 121(80.7) expressed that they get informed regularly about the availability of GL in their libraries. This shows the positive response of the library in disseminating information about GL.

5.3.17 Organization of GL in the library: The organisation of literature in the libraries will influence the identification, access and use of GL. Therefore an attempt has been made here to elicit the views regarding the convenient arrangement of GL. The below mentioned methods are practiced by different libraries in the organisation as mentioned in table 17 to facilitate the use of GL.

1. Classificationwise
2. Accessionwise and
3. Institution wise

Table 17. Organisation in the Library

Acc.No Wise	*Classification wise*	*Institution wise*	*Any other*	*O(notresponded)*
21(14)	89(59.3)	8(5.3)	30(20)	2(1.3)

Table 18. Arrangement in the Library

Along with books	*Separately*	*Mixed*	*O (Notresponded)*	*Total*
64(42.7)	70(46.7)	14(9.3)	2 (1.3)	150

Table 19. Convenience of Arrangement

Yes	*No*	*Total*
135(90)	15(10)	150

5.3.18 Arrangement in the Library : Majority of the respondents 135(90%) opined that the arrangement of grey literature followed in the libraries is satisfactory as mentioned in table 19. All the methods mentioned about are found to be convenient to the users in their own way . Each method has its own advantages and disadvantages. Based on the experience they chose the method of arrangement as indicated in table 18.

The below mentioned table 20 shows the extent of satisfaction felt by the respondents about arrangement followed in their libraries.

Table 20. Extent of satisfaction about arrangement

0-25	*26-50*	*51-75*	*76-100*	*00 (not responded)*	*Total*
21(14)	55(36.7)	38(25.3)	6(4.3)	30(20)	150

5.3.19 Optimum Use of GL : First law of Library science states that books are for use. This is applicable to GL. The libraries should strive to see that optimum use of every resource, including GL. The special nature of GL makes the library professional to identify ways and methods of organizing the GL, which enables the user to identify and access. Such a situation will contribute to the enhancement of the extensive use of GL. This will satisfy the second and third law of Library Science.

The respondents have expressed their opinions about the methods to be adopted for organization and dissemination of GL. The following suggestions were given by the respondents for the optimum use of GL.

* **Use of IT**: If computers available with internet connectivity the use of GL can be made optimal.
* **Timely Access**: Occasional papers, annual reports, statistical documents should be made accessible in time.
* **Contacts with other Libraries**: The librarian should develop contacts with other organisations to get the GL regularly.
* **Organisation**: Organise GL as a separate collection.
* **Subject bibliographies**: Prepare subject bibliographies of GL
* **Dissemination mechanism**: Proper dissemination mechanism, about the availability of GL should be developed using Current Awareness Services, Selective Dissemination services etc. Circulate the GL information to all the staff immediately.
* **Acquisition policy**: The librarian should prepare a policy to systematically acquire GL GL should be collected regularly which is available but scattered locally and regionally by writing regularly to the concerned organisations/institutions GL
* **Exchange Policy**: Attempts should be made to get more GL on exchange basis

The suggestions given above, if implemented may create an impact on the optimum use of GL. Therefore the libraries should evaluate the suggestions and examine the feasibility to enable them to implement most of the suggestions given by the respondents.

5.3.20 Publications of institutions : GL is published by a number of organisations. The researcher looked for the publications of the organisations which deal with subjects relevant to them. It helps to know the awareness level of the social scientists, and how they are familiar with the organisations relevant to their subject field. It also helps the librarian in collection development by providing details about the documents where they are published, where available, how to get etc. The following table 21 shows the number of institutions known by the respondents which generate GL relevant to their needs regularly.

Table 21. Publications of Institutions known

1 (Upto 5)	*2* (6-10)	*3* (10+)
91(60.7)	31(20.7)	28(18.7)

About 91 (60.7%) of the respondents know at least five institutions whose GL is relevant to their work. Further the data shows that the respondents are frequently using the publications of the International organizations like World Bank, ODI, WHO, UNICEF and Asian Development Bank, and national organisations like National Institute of Rural Development(NIRD, Hyderabad), National Agricultural Bank for Rural Development (NABARD, Bombay) , National Remote Sensing Agency (NRSA, Hyderabad), National Institute of Nutrition (NIN, Hyderabad) and Indian Council of Social Science Research (ICSSR, New Delhi), and Regional organizations like Institute for Social and Economic Change (ISEC, Bangalore), Madras Institute of Development Studies (MIDS, Madras), Centre for development Studies (CDS, Trivandram), State Institute of Rural Development (SIRDs) Publications, Institute of Rural Management, Anand (IRMA, Gujarat) publications, local organizations like Centre for Economic and Social Science (CESS, Hyderabad), Universities, Institute of Public Enterprise (IPE, Hyderabad), National Institute of Agricultural Extension Management (MANAGE, Hyderabad) and Administrative Staff College of India(ASCI, Hyderabad). As the number of institutions grow to more than ten, the awareness levels drop. Hence the organizations should try to create their web sites to make their GL more visible. This will also increase the accessibility to the users to improve the use more GL documents. Because of the limited awareness of respondents about the institutions that generate GL the researcher felt that lack of awareness and accessibility are the barriers for optimum use of GL. Some of the suggestions could be as follows:

(1) user education to familarise with the publications produced by different social science organisations.

(2) introduction of information services like CAS and SDI in GL

(3) organisation of the exhibitions of GL.

5.3.21 Internet: The explosive growth of the internet and the world wide web(www) in recent years has an impact on almost every field of human activity . While its effect on librarianship is more intensive owing to the fact that internet influences on the library profession. Internet is one important tool which is used to surf the cyber space for information. Internet is the network of networks. A variety of information is available on internet to identify and access the required information through search engines like Excite, Hotbot, Yahoo, Alta Vista. They search the web sites by using the utilities like web, images, groups and directory and gives the required information. The following table 22 indicates the number of respondents using the internet.

Table 22. Internet use

Yes	*No*	*Total*
106(70.6)	44(29.3)	150

One hundred and six (70.6%) respondents are familiar with the Internet. They are using Internet either at office, residence or at the cyber café. The year 2000 was known as year of Internet. During the last two years the number of Internet users have increased enormously. In spite of that only 70.6% of social scientists are using Internet as a tool for information access. More use of Internet influence effective use of GL.

Limited information on social sciences is being generated in developing countries like India. It may increase in near future with the use of IT by Social Science Institutions. The NGOs are working on various problems at grassroots level and generating enormous literature. NGOs play an important role to satisfy the information needs of the social scientists. Recently many institutions including NGOs like BAIF, Aghakan Foundation, AFARM are having their web sites and put their information, activities and publications directly onto the web. The INDEV (India Development) website is encouraging and helping the NGOS to create their own web pages for their visibility. These developments would enhance the use of GL generated by many NGOs.

Table 23. Internet Accessibility

At Office	*At Residence*	*At Outside*	*Total*
59(55.6)	38(35.8)	9(8.4)	106

The above table 23 infers that majority of the respondents are able to surf internet either at office or at residence. The respondents felt that the information available on electronic media is more than that of the print media. This is not unusual in the wake of developments that are taking place in IT. Though 44 (29.3) respondents do not use the internet probably they may likely to use internet in due course.

About 90(60%) respondents opined that the internet is helping them to access more GL like conference proceedings, research reports, thesis etc. They also feel they got satisfied with the information available on internet. 98(65.3%) respondents are satisfied to the extent of 50% about the information available on internet. Hence, it can be inferred that the institutions should get equipped with the Internet and publicise their GL to facilitate the users to access more GL.

5.3.21.1 Networks : Any network aims at evolving a mechanism of partnership in which each member has something useful to contribute to others in the network. The goals of networking provide positive effect on the library user in terms of access to more materials and services mainly resource sharing is the focal point of library networking.

Library networks are one of the tools aimed at increasing availability, accessibility and thus utilization of information. Several long-range initiatives have been taken by various organizations like NICNET, INDONET, CALIBNET, DELNET, INFLIBNET, ERNET, PUNENET etc. though some of these networks are not fully in operation. Also many institutions are designing and developing their own web sites. Libraries are using the email facility for exchange of information and through telnet the users are accessing the remote databases.

5.3.21.2 Access to networks : There are instances where networks complement the internet. The combined effect of the library network and the internet would enhance the access to GL. Unfortunately in the study area of Hyderabad there is no such local network. There appears to be email facilities only that too in not all libraries.

Table 24 Access to Networks

Yes	*No*	*Total*
89(593)	61(40.7)	150

Majority of respondents (59.3) have expressed that they are aware about the usefulness of the library networks as shown in table 24. And also have knowledge about the bibliographic databases. A number of databases are accessible through telephone lines.

5.3.22 Information System for GL (GLIS) : The respondents felt that there is a need for a separate database for GL in all libraries and subsequently develop links to all the participating libraries to take advantage of the database. They suggested the following steps, to create networks of libraries for making optimum use of GL. (1). First they have to identify the libraries of similar interest. (2). The GL data should be developed as a computer based database by individual libraries. (3). These databases must be made available through internet or should be web based. (4) The access must be made available to every library/user.

Many respondents have strongly agreed to the suggestion of networking of institutions in accessing GL, as mentioned in table 25.

Table 25. Need for Networking

0	*Strongly Agree*	*Agree*	*Disagree*	*Not Agree*	*Total*
3(2)	87(58)	58(38.7)	1(.7)	1(.7)	150

Table 26. Need for GL information system (GLIS)

Yes	*No*	*Total*
129(86)	21(14)	150

The respondents apparently need a specialized information system for GL, which facilitates to select and communicate the documents from the points of their generation and making them available to the users. It provides information specifically, thoroughly and present in a manner most convenient to the user at a reasonable expense. The system is supposed to provide a current and comprehensive view of what is being done, where, how and when. Such information system if available for a subject like GL, it would be more useful to the research community.

The proposed Grey Literature Information System (GLIS) will provide bibliographical information of GL i.e, the details of documents available in the participating organizations. All the information will be stored in the computer at GLIS. The key word search and document type search could be provided against payment or through a password. The cost of photocopying, mailing could be charged by the institutions. The respondents stated that the development of GLIS is essential in order to get awareness and access to the GL in their relevant fields of study (Table 26).

Table 27. Establishment of GLIS

0	*Local*	*Regional*	*National*	*Total*
16(10.7)	19(12.7)	88(58.7)	27(18)	150

Majority of the respondents viewed that the networking should be at regional level , If it is difficult to start straight away at the regional level, it would be better if the networking is done at local level and extend later to regional level and further extend to national level as an ideal implementation strategy. This statement is more emphasized by them due to the reason that social science subject by its very nature differs on the basis of ethnic group, language, society and community

Table 28. Usage of GL

Not responded	*Not Used*	*Marginally*	*Substantially*
10(6.7)	12(8)	84(56)	44(29.3)

Respondents were requested to give their opinion regarding the extent of use of GL by them. 84 (56) respondents opined that it is being used marginally, substantially by 44 (29.3), and not used by 12 respondents as indicated in table 28.

When the respondents were asked to give appropriate reasons for marginal use they indicated reasons like Lack of awareness, lack of accessibility, lack of Bibliographical control, lack of availability, and organisational deficiency etc.

Optimum use of GL is possible only when the above problems are solved. Awareness and accessibility are the main problems. Some measures as suggested in the preceding pages, which may be attempted on should be taken to overcome these problems based on the qualitative answers of the respondents.

5.3.23 Information Technology and use of GL : With the advent of information technology, apart from books and journals, the library has to deal with other information media like CD-ROMs and databases. The specialized collection of GL increases with these materials. Apart from print media, audiocassettes, videocassettes, films, filmstrips, magnetic tapes etc emerged in the era of information technology. The networking gave birth to a global village with the help of internet. This media and internet plays an important role in creating awareness, accessibility in the use of GL.

Table 29. Information Technology and Use of Grey Literature

Not responded	*Very Strongly Agree*	*Agree*	*Disagree*	*Not at all agree*
6(4.0)	81(54)	60(40)	3(2)	0

81 (54) respondents very strongly agree that the advances in Information Technology would enhance the use of GL, followed by 60 (40) agree, only three have disagreed, no respondent said that not at all agree. Majority of the respondents (141) expressed that IT would help in creating awareness, improve accessibility/availability and to enhance the usage of GL.

Based on the citation analysis of JRD and the data on use pattern of GL, we can conclude that the GL is found to be an important information source and it is being used by social scientists for different purposes. Lack of bibliographical control and lack of accessibility are the main barriers which hinders the use of GL completely. There is a need to have a Grey Literature Information System (GLIS)by using the electronic networks which enables the social scientists to make enhanced use of GL. The proposed model of GLIS is presented in the next chapter (5).

5.4 References

Ramadevi, T (1999): Paper presented in the Fourth International Conference on Grey Literature. New Frontiers in Grey Literature at Washington, D.C during 4-5th October 1999.

6
Grey Literature Information System in Social Science : A model

GL is an essential source for academic, research and other activities. There is a need to provide access to GL, to enable the researcher to keep up to date in his field. GL covers universe of subjects in all the segments of knowledge. It serves the information needs of various people from different disciplines. Despite being of great importance to researchers, such information has often been found hard to identify and access as it is undervalued. Effective dissemination could be made possible if an information system in the area of GL is planned with an objective to create awareness and access to information sources.

6.1 Information System

An information system aims to facilitate selection and communication of ideas from the point of their generation to that of making them available to the users. It provides information specifically, thoroughly and expeditiously. The system presents information in a most convenient manner to the user at a reasonable expense. Its aim is to make the best use of the resources. The Information system should be able to provide a current , updated and comprehensive view of what is being done, where , how and by whom. It should be able to help planners and decision makers decide what ought to be done in the future. The system should be action-based and as far as possible mission-oriented and it must be designed so as to overcome the many kinds of obstacles which normally related to the flow of information. A good information system must be interactive, dynamic, and capable of modification keeping the changing needs in mind with minimum of cost and with greatest of speed and reliability.

As we have seen earlier networks facilitated obtaining of all kinds of published and unpublished information. In near future networks may substitute for traditional information media such as published journals, libraries and online databases. Networked publishing using electronic networks for the dissemination of documents can significantly improve awareness, accessibility and availability besides the quality of information services and therefore enhances the value of information.

6.2 Need for GLIS

There are a number of information systems designed in different subjects like Rural Development Information System, Agricultural Information System , Medical Information System, Educational Information System etc. All these systems are subject oriented. However an information system for GL in social science thoroughly oriented to type of literature will be an advantageous. These systems would be able to provide information in all the respective subjects. As we have seen from the analysis of data obtained through our questionnaire there is a wealth of potentially useful, relevant and much needed, locally generated information but there are barriers to its access and availability due to poor knowledge of its existence, poor bibliographical control, underestimation of its value, lack of information policy on GL, budgetary constraints . To overcome these problems we need to have a Grey Literature Information System (GLIS) to act as a one stop location for GL. The GLIS should create a platform for mutual and fruitful co-existence of all the GL producers. Its main job is to network the institutions of similar interest and facilitate the exchange of information among these institutions.

6.3 Issues and Development of GLIS

GLIS has to be developed with an important objective to provide bibliographical information of GL documents available in the participating organisatioons, while the responsibility of access and document delivery will remain with the participating organisations. In this context there are number of issues that need to be thoroughly examined.

1. The coverage may be limited to social sciences.
2. Document Delivery should be left to the participating Organisation.
3. The data should be provided on a standardised format.
4. All the information will be stored in the computer at GLIS
5. The keyword search and document type search will be provided against payment to non participating institutions and against a password to participating institutions.
6. Institutions which do not have computerised system or access to the Internet facility, may be encouraged to have the facility soon and in the meantime correspondence with GLIS by post and get the necessary information.
7. The document delivery will be on payment basis the terms for which will be decided by the individual participating organisations.
8. The cost of photocopying, mailing expenses will be charged by the institutions, when they will dispatch the documents to the desired destination.
9. As some GL varieties are of transient nature, participating institutions should make the database updated by constantly checking the same and withdrawing the obsolete and transient literature.
10. The Manpower should get advanced training to manage the specialized system.

6.4 Networking and IT

To develop GLIS, the information technology has to be

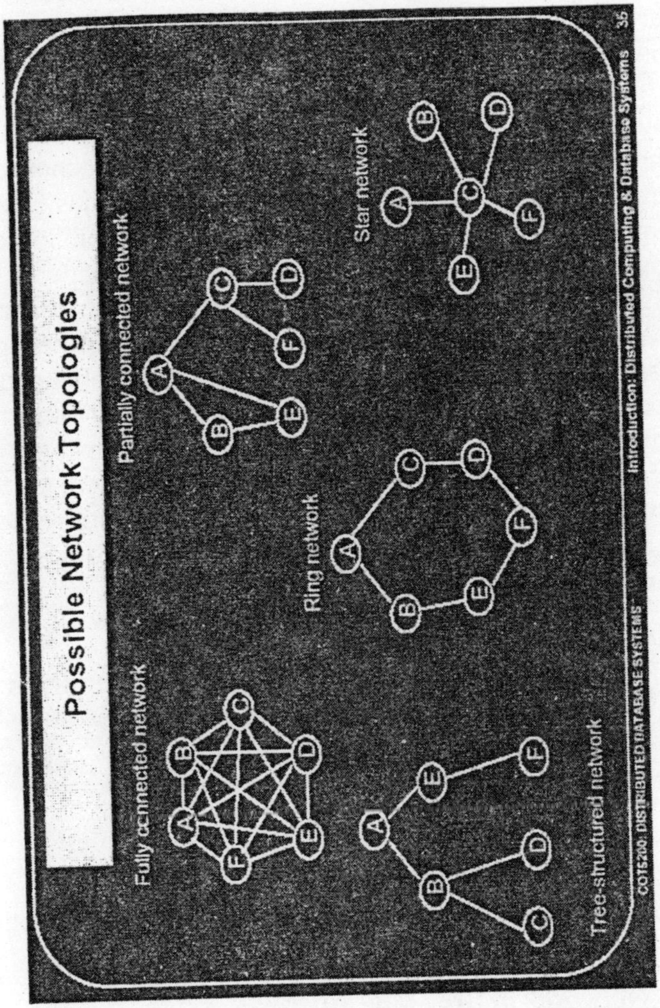
Possible Network Topologies
Fully connected network
Partially connected network
Ring network
Star network
Tree-structured network
COTS200: DISTRIBUTED DATABASE SYSTEMS
Introduction: Distributed Computing & Database Systems

used as a tool. By using IT, a network has to be developed in order to access the information available even remotely. This network as mentioned earlier provides several advantages. The concept of network aims at evolving a mechanism of partnership in which each member has something useful to contribute to the others in the network. In the context of library/ information services, network consists of information users, sources, programmes and projects with links between them. Though the idea of a network is not new, the emergence of new information and communication technologies has given an impetus and an urgency. The Inter-library loan or bibliographic exchange in any form is the chef justification of a network (Rab, S.F., 1994). Growing awareness for the need for resource sharing, the all round resource storage, an increase in computer installations, an access facility in libraries, an enhanced skill base and improved telecommunication facility within and across the geographical regions have been responsible for the recent spurt in library networking activities (Lahari, A. 1997). In modern information networks, technology is utilised to link libraries, specialised data resources, or individuals to the persons or institutions in need of information.

6.5 Characteristics of a Network

1. Information resources-collection of documents and databases for data in whatever Medium.
2. Users-usually remote from the main sources of information.
3. Formal organizations of cooperating, representing of different databases and/or groups of users.
4. Methods of dissemination of information or the delivery of resources to users.

6.6 Networks in Grey Literature

Most of the networks were initially designed to cover only science and technology. IFLIBNET is an exception because it is to cover university libraries which are usually multi-disciplinary. DELNET also has some participants from social sciences and humanities. There are some international networks for GL like Greynet and European GL in European countries: SIGLE, EAGLE.

6.6.1 Grey Net : Grey Net is providing information about the conferences on GL., It prepares bibliographies of GL documents, it releases a newsletter periodically. It also gives the list of publications on GL It brought out the international guide to persons and organizations in grey literature, which includes the address of the institutions who are members of the Grey Net along with their grey literature products. Grey Net is also trying to bring out the international journal on GL, including articles relating to the studies, surveys conducted in greyliterature.. It also provides information about research and developments in the area of GL. It is inviting the libraries to become partners in the network which facilitates free flow of GL among the user community.

6.6.2 EAGLE and SIGLE : The mission of the European Association for Grey Literature Exploitation (EAGLE) is to provide access to, and promote the use of, grey literature produced in European countries by encouraging co-operation between interested information and document supply centers. The database SIGLE is available online through STN international and BLAISE. A CD-ROM version of SIGLE is available from Silver-Platter Information Ltd. The SIGLE tapes are also available for leasing by organizations for their own use or for merging with other products by agreement with EAGLE. SIGLE covers all subject fields and all types of grey literature.

All documents listed are available from or through the national center which entered the records in the SIGLE database. Copies can be ordered directly from the source cited in the document reference or through (inter) national interlibrary networks. SIGLE covers all subject fields and all types of grey literature. There are national SIGLE centers in Belgium, Denmark, France, Germany, Hungary, Italy, Latvia, Luxembourg. The Netherlands, Portugal, Russia, Slovakia, Spain, United Kingdom. English language descriptions of Russian grey literature with abstracts are loaded into SIGLE.

6.7 Creation of databases

The databases have to be developed before networking the institutions. The creation of databases may vary depends on the need and purpose. There are two popular methods that being followed for creation of databases one is Distributed database another is centralized database. Let us examine them in detail.

6.8 Distributed Database

6.8.1 Definition : A distributed database (DDB) is one in which the data is contained within a number of separate subsystems, usually in different physical locations. If the constituent sub-systems are essentially similar, the system is said to be homogeneous, otherwise it is said to be heterogeneous. DDB may vary considerably.

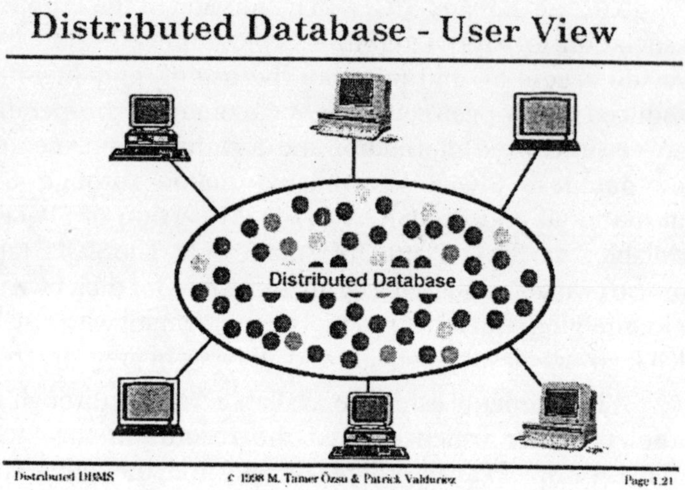

6.8.2 Distributed Database Management System : A distributed database is a collection of multiple, logically interrelated databases distributed over a computer network. A system that runs on a collection of machines that don't have shared memory, yet looks to its users like a single computer. All machines run the same kernel. Each kernel controls its own resources. A Data Management System is the (D_DBMS) software that manages the DDB and provides an access mechanism that makes this distribution transparent to the users. A distributed database is a collection of data that belongs logically to the same system but is physically spread over the sites of a computer network. Local data is locally owned and managed with local accountability with security considerations and integrity considerations.

6.8.3 Factors that led to the development of DDBS

1. Distributed nature of data
2. Increased reliability and availability of information
3. Data sharing while maintaining some measure of local control
4. Improved performance

6.8.4 Advantages : Local autonomy, no reliance on a central site, continuous operation, location independence, distributed query, processing, distributed transaction management, hardware independence, operating system independence, network Independence, are some of the advantages of DDBs.

6.8.5 Limitations

1. All operations at a given site are controlled by that site.
2. In some situations some slight loss of autonomy is inevitable.
3. Fragmentation problem
4. Replication problem
5. Update of replicated relation
6. Multiple-site integrity constraint problem

6.9 Centralised Database (CDB)

A database system which resides at one of the nodes of a network of computers is a centralized database

6.9.1 Functions of CDB

1. To access remote sites and transmit queries and data

among in various sites via a communication network.

2. To keep track of the data distribution and replication in the DDBMS catalog
3. To devise execution strategies for queries
4. To decide on which copy of a replicated data item.
5. To maintain the consistency of copies of a replicated data item.
6. To recover from individual site crashes and from new types of failures such as failure of a communication link.

Reliance on a central site would be undesirable for at least the following two reasons

The central site might be a bottleneck, the system would be vulnerable to unexpected failures of communication lines

6.10 How to network

There are different methods of accessing the database. Number one option is to develop homepage of GLIS and make its database web-enabled. Number two option is to put the GLIS database on the GLIS own server and number three option is to host the GLIS database in any of the national networks like NIC, ICSSR

6.11 Responsibilities

There are many responsibilities assigned to a network manager of GLIS. Responsibility of maintaining/updating the assigned databases in the standard formats Update the bibliographical records continuously. Take into consideration the issues related to copyright, proprietary rights, licensing and security of Information. Will have obligation to make sure that all the listed documents are available at the location mentioned in each record. Providing information on request to the networking members. Sending a copy of local database for purposes of maintaining central database

Pricing of identified services reasonably. Responding to queries within a reasonable time. The generator or author should inform the GLIS if they publish any GL document in conventional form. Will have obligation to make sure that all the listed documents are available at the location mentioned in each record. All the participating institutions should enter into an MOU stating the responsibilities, liabilities and commitment of the participating institutions like updating of the bibliographical records periodically, develop infrastructural facilities, provide availability status of GL documents from among the participating institutions, provision of access to GL documents by the means as specified in the records (ILL, Photocopying), provide the document delivery service on actual cost basis, inform the GLIS if they publish any GL document in conventional form, exploit the information by participating organisations available through GLIS indiscriminately for commercial purpose.

6.12 GLIS for Social Sciences

Based on the data received from the social scientists and the librarians the researcher felt the need for establishment of GLIS. There are number of social science institutions working in India, and a lot of GL information is emerging from these institutions. It is difficult for the social scientists to know what GL information is available in which library. If we have a network like GLIS it will facilitate the accessibility and availability of GL and enhance its use. It also helps to overcome the problems relating to the lack of bibliographical control and lack of accessibility which are the main causes for the marginal use of GL. Establishment of GLIS is essential to enhance the use of GL substantially and completely. Initially the network should be initiated with the 9 institutions in the first phase and may be extended further in the 2nd phase, to other institutions.

6.13 Objectives of GLIS

1. To increase the level of awareness about the information content in the GL.
2. To make the bibliographic records of GL available to the participating institutions, in order to improve the accessibility.

3. To encourage participating institutions to provide inputs to the GLIS
4. To facilitate effective GL document delivery among the participating institutions.
5. To maintain computerised information system for quick retrieval of information on GL documents.

While planning and designing the GLIS, the involvement of the librarians of the participating organizations, administrative and the technical staff is essential. The feasibility plan of the GLIS should be developed. After finalisation the plan should be approved by the Administration for its implement action.

The selected nine organisations are specialised in their own way. The universities are dealing with different departments covering various subjects in the universe of knowledge. Social sciences is one of them. Among the selected social science organisations in Hyderabad, the researcher suggested that the National Institute of Rural Development (NIRD) may take the initiative to coordinate the other eight institutions, because it is one of the biggest Research and Training Institutions in social sciences and also developed a huge database on rural development an interdisciplinary subject of social science. It also developed a virtual library on rural development by providing links to various organisations on the internet. The activities of NIRD are discussed below in detail. It is suggested that the participating institutions should send the bibliographical details of GL documents to NIRD on regular basis. NIRD can inturn bring out the holdings list periodically and distribute to other libraries which help them to know the existence, availability and accessibility of GL in the participating libraries. This can perhaps pave the way to enhance the use of GL by social scientists.

6.14 Role of NIRD in Social Science Information System

National Institute of Rural Development (NIRD) is an apex research, training and consultancy institution in rural development sector. One of the major functions of NIRD is to collect, document and disseminate rural development information pertaining not only to India but also other developing countries for the use of development community. In its endeavor to achieve this, NIRD makes continuous efforts to develop and strengthen its information resource base relating to rural development and allied aspects.. As a result, NIRD has developed a strong database of development literature. Centre on Rural Documentation (CORD) established as a plan scheme during Sixth Plan, is a one-stop location in India for development literature. CORD has computerised its total database of books and journal articles. Presently the computerised database consists of nearly 1.70 lakh references. In keeping with the advancements in information technology, NIRD has made efforts to upgrade its information handling capabilities.

6.14.1 Computerised Library and Information Clearinghouse: With a view to further streamline the collection and flow of information, NIRD has set-up a Computerised Library and Information Clearinghouse (CLIC) for rural development. The facility is intended to cater to the information needs of the development community consisting of policy makers, planners, functionaries, researchers, trainers at the ministries, SIRDs and other research and training institutions at national and international level who have rural development as their focus. The uniqueness of CLIC is that it provides information on different aspects of rural development at one single point which can be accessed by the development community world wide. Different databases / information presently available through CLIC under various broad categories are made web enabled thus making its access versatile. The following databases are available currently under CLIC.

6.14.2 General Information : Information on policy documents, circulars, and other such publications of various institutions, list of rural development schemes, rural development institutions, rural development experts, full text of the NIRD publication 'Rural Development Statistics'. Who is who in the Ministry along with their telephone, fax and address, Rural Development Programmes Operationalised by the central government, Rural Development Programmes designed by the respective states, success stories in rural development, National and International Institutions, Data Banks etc.

6.14.3 Training : Besides NIRD training programmes, list of institutions, both national and international, including SIRDs offering training.

6.14.4 Research : Information relating to on-going research and completed research projects of NIRD and other institutions, and Research Highlights of the projects completed

6.14.5 Publications : Full texts of the current issues of NIRD Newsletter, and contents page of the current issue of the Journal of Rural Development, publications catalogue, etc.,

6.14.6 Library Database : Provides access to CORD library database of 1.70 lakh references, current issues of CORD publications, list of journals subscribed in CORD, Rural Development Institutions in India, Non Governmental Organisations (NGO), Funding agencies, Ready Reference, Libraries allover the world etc

The collection of above kinds of data involves expertise in identifying sources and linking those sources virtually with NIRD. Such an expertise is useful in managing GLIS. As NIRD is the main source in social science information in Hyderabad, it can perhaps act as a central coordination unit for all other 8 institutions to participate in the proposed GLIS.

The proposed model considering the focus of the activities of the participating institutions will cater to the information needs of social scientists in different specialisations like management development, agricultural information, agricultural extension and management, public and small scale enterprises , social sciences in general, rural development and allied aspects. As the institutions specialised in the above areas of activities they can be the nodal points in the respective fields in the proposed network. The detailed information about the participating institutions is given in the institutional profiles , in the anexure No. To achieve the above they should be perfect understanding among the participating institutions. Ways and means like signing of MOU can be explored to achieve the objectives.

Proposed model of GLIS

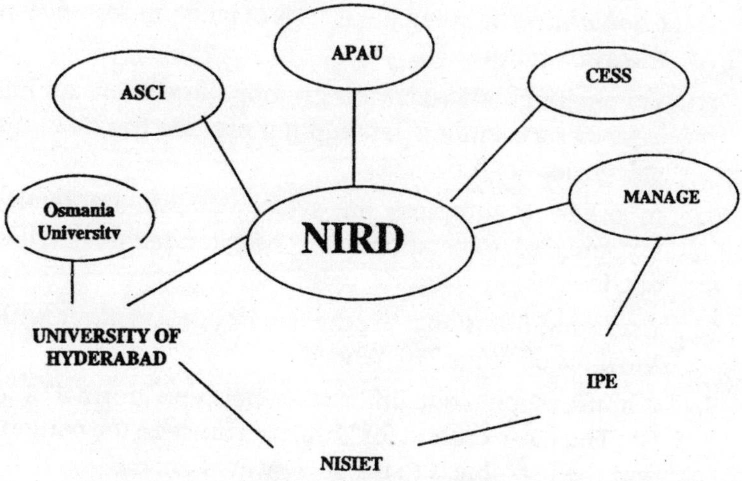

Fig 8

Note: The interconnections are to be seen as two-way connections between each institute with other. Though the netwoik iecommended following star format, for the sake of clarity, the interconnections between all the participating institutions with each other could not be shown

6.15 Proposed model of GLIS

The above diagram gives the proposed model for GLIS where the 9 institutions together networked in a star format and to realise the objectives stated above. The responsibility of each member of the network is also outlined earlier for successful operation of GLIS.

6.16 Success of an information system for GL depends upon

1. If the information content of the GL products are of some

use to others, the individuals and organisational producers of GL should be recognised and appreciated.

2. Their willingness to provide copies of the documents to designated pools May have to be ascertained. It is also necessary to understand the attitudes of both the producers and the potential consumers towards the GL.

3. In all countries national systems for the availability of GL nay have to be created.

   Cooperation between libraries is of great importance in the availability of GL.

4. The legal regulations covering national and international inter-library lending should not exclude the different categories of GL.

5. In order to complete the system of availability the exchange of publications must be extended to all types of GL.

6. Users and librarians require a compilation along with the lines of "What" is "Where"

7. Libraries should not differentiate between "normal" and GL. The basic criteria for librarians must be the content and the usefulness to the society or clientele.

8. GL requires a minimum standard of bibliographic description.

6.16 Conclusions

A very large percentage of information from GL documents remain unnoticed or under the roof of a single organization. There is a scatter of ever-growing stockpile of information in GL documents, which have an important role in information transfer. Unless organizations which generate them and collect them, bring this literature to the notice of the readers, it will remain buried in the collection through it has a strong potential intrinsic value. Networked publishing using electronic networking for the dissemination of documents can significantly improve the quality of information services and therefore enhance the value of information. This is especially true for information which is not readily available through traditional publishing channels. The establishment of the GLIS will be the first step at local level for organizing GL produced in the country. It can later become part of an regional, national and international network.

6.17 References

Gokhale, P.A (1999) : Information system for grey literature in India: A model . *Library Science with Slant to Documentation and Information Studies*, 36(4) ,229-236p.

Lahari, A (1997) : Libraries and Information Services; South Asia in World Information Report 1997-98. Paris : UNESCO, 33 to 45 P.

Own, M.J.S (1993) : Value and use of grey literature :The implications of networking publishing . Ist International Conference on Grey Literature. Amesterdam:. TransAtlantic, 308-319p.

Rab, S.F (1994) : The Canging Frontiers of Library and Information Science. New Delhi: Commonwealth publishers, 39p.

Ramadevi, T (1988) : Use of grey literature in doctoral dissertations of the A.NGR Agricultural University (1982-88): MLISC Dissertation. Waltair : Andhra University. 85p.

7
Summary and Conclusions

7.1 Introduction

Information is considered as one of the basic needs of human being. After the invention of printing press, and as a consequence of mission oriented researches carried out in various institutions, Universities and other public and private organisations, the information is now presented in different formats like books, journals, reports, thesis etc. The information is transferred from one person to another person from one place to another place through various media. There are two types of information sources one is documentary and another is non-documentary. The documentary sources may be categorized as primary, secondary and tertiary . The primary sources are most important for research. They help the researcher to keep himself up-to-date and well informed of the latest in his field. By its nature, the primary literature is widely scattered , and it is difficult to locate . As a result the secondary and tertiary literature sources emerged to have a control over the primary literature.

Social sciences constitute an important branch of human sciences. It studies a particular category of human phenomena in its social and cultural environment. The second chapter discussed in detail about the subjects that come under social sciences, development of social sciences in India, role of ICSSR in promoting social science research, emergence of funding agencies for research in social sciences, social science information generating agencies, information seeking behaviour of the social scientists etc.

Libraries collect various information sources for the users. There are conventional and non conventional documents. Libraries give priority for the published documents which are under bibliographical control, compared to Grey Literature (GL).

As dealt in the third chapter, grey literature covers all segments of knowledge , it serves the information needs of various people from different disciplines. DEVISIS study report (1976) mentioned that the 60% of the literature in social sciences is grey which is produced in limited quantity, for a limited purpose and not available through regular trade channels and consequently not come under the bibliographic control. Due to this problem most of the literature generated in the social sciences is not being used. Hence there is a need to study the problems faced by the social scientists to access and use of GL.

The researcher made an attempt to study the use pattern of GL by social scientists, not only by administering a structured questionnaire to elicit their ideas but also applied citation analysis method to determine the use pattern of grey literature. The questions included in the canvassed questionnaire relating to the type of information sources used, how they buildup their personal collection, how the libraries are arranging the GL and tackle the problems of the readers in accessing the GL , their knowledge about the internet and other networks etc. Out of 200 questionnaires a total of 150 filled in questionnaires were received. The questionnaires were analysed qualitatively and quantitatively. The results were discussed in the fourth chapter.

The analysis concluded that the respondents felt the need for establishment of Grey Literature Information System (GLIS) in social sciences in Hyderabad. They also felt that there should be a policy for acquiring GL material for the libraries and also stated that a separate database of GL is to be developed in all the libraries and promote the resource sharing among the libraries. Chapter five dealt with the proposed model of GLIS, its components, responsibilities, objectives etc.

7.2 Suggestions

Based on the qualitative and quantitative data the following suggestions emerged.

1. There is no doubt that GL becomes an important component of the literature for any research. Given the fact that it contains valuable information which is very useful to planners and decision makers, GL may have to be treated just as conventional literature. A policy for collecting and disseminating GL should be formulated. Because of the nature and characteristics of GL it needs more special treatment than conventional literature. Its collection and organisation should be given the importance it deserves by the concerned institutions.
2. The most practical approach is the establishment of a clear government policy on GL by the national government. Such a policy is no doubt bound to compel producers to deposit copies of their work with gazetted repository institutions. In India with substantial numbers of producers, it may be advisable to appoint more than one institution at regional and local levels as repository centers.
3. The first step is to have an inventory of actual and potential producers of GL within the country. Having identified the producers it will be necessary to sensitize them on the need to deposit at least a copy of their publications to a designated depository centre within the country. In addition, each producer should be encouraged to maintain a textual data bank of all their publications as well as a bibliographic database on internet for making it visible for actual and potential users
4. Learned societies, as major producers of GL, have a crucial role to play given the fact that they are in a position to monitor all the activities that will generate GL. Thus apart from depositing a copy of all their publications with the designated depository centre in the country , it is necessary for each learned society to maintain a small documentation centre in which all publications including GL that emanate from the society will be collected, organised and disseminated. It will not be difficult for them to abstract such documents and make

such abstracts available to potential users, either directly or through internet.

5. Organisers of GL have to use unconventional means to learn about and acquire their material which often exists in formats that have been difficult to obtain, handle, and disseminate. They have to maintain a closer connection with their authors and producers than is customary. With these closer connections to their user community, GL managers would be able to learn more about how information is used in their fields and to find out from their users more about their unmet information needs. Librarians have an opportunity to play a vital role in organizing traditional and non-traditional information-whether black, grey or white-into an organized and coherent "virtual library" for their researchers and users.

6. The Internet can be a very useful medium for disseminating GL to users. Producers of GL can provide bibliographic access to their publications by using the internet to publicise the publications. Institutions and individuals with experience in GL collection, organization, and access are uniquely qualified to bring order through internet information resources. Working within the world of GL, one must often forge new solutions and operate with little traditional infrastructure or precedent. This is partly true because GL has been traditionally ignored by established information managers such as libraries and publishers.

7. Internet offers authors a new medium of scientific and technical communication, and new paradigms of communication are emerging . We should take that the information world is changing and that the information sources, and particularly GL, are likely to become increasingly electronic. Nevertheless, problems related to bibliographic control of GL will not be solved only by using new technologies. Therefore appropriate standards for successful identification and easy access to desired information will be more and more necessary.

8. Advances in information and communication technologies have resulted in the creation of enormous electronic networks that indicate geographic and social barriers are now becoming less of an obstacle in information communication. Needless to say that where information technology has been effectively used as a tool and channel for information generation and communication, the inevitable production of GL and grey information is on the increase. Mention can be made of digital libraries which are also not under bibliographic control, thus remain grey in terms of bibliographic control and systematic access.
9. The proper collection, storage processing and creating access to GL is dependent on a well established National Information Infrastructure. The difficulty in organizing, disseminating and utilization of GL stems from the weak national information infrastructures. Embarking upon the strengthening of existing National Information Infrastructures to fit into Global Electronic Networks. Sensitization programme for users of the importance of GL may have to be considered.
10. Using electronic networks for the dissemination of GL has potential benefits, which increase the value of institutional publications both at the end- user and to the institution itself. If network publishing continues to develop, it will lead to an increase in both the production and use of GL.
11. Special efforts are necessary to control the newly emerging GL like meta documents, CDs, tapes, videos etc.,
12. The networked future of GL will stimulate the transformation of libraries from collection- based to access-based institutions. Libraries will have to acquire new skills in order to make this change, and will have to become involved in the major developments in the field of networked information resources.

13. To overcome the problems of poor bibliographical control, lack of accessibility and availability, we need to have a Grey Literature Information system (GLIS) to act as a one stop location for GL.
14. The participating institutions should ensure the effective functioning of the proposed model of GLIS by entering into an Memorandom Of Understanding (MOU) relating to the responsibilities, liabilities and commitment.
15. National level agency such as NASSDOC should take responsibility in establishing a network of social science agencies generating and acquiring the GL in social science.
16. NASSDOC as a national organization should develop a national database of GL like SIGLE in Europe.
17. Communication channels have to be developed between the social science organizations to share GL resources
18. ICSSR should help the social science organizations financially in the library automation process for enhanced resource sharing.
19. National Institute of Rural Development may coordinate the proposed model of GLIS in Hyderabad .

7.3 Conclusions

GL covers almost every field of knowledge. Some varieties are liable to be superseded in their content over a period of time, yet they are not easily replaceable. Their availability largely depends upon the policy of the generating institutions, which may exercise their authority for whether or not all the documents should be made public knowledge. But their existence should be known. There is a tremendous output of knowledge through GL variety and librarians should take a pragmatic approach towards it. The acquisition, processing, dissemination should be a part of strategies that might be employed to capture this fluid form of literature.

Network publishing using electronic networking for the dissemination of documents can significantly improve the quality of information services and therefore enhance the value of information. This is especially true for information which is not readily available through traditional publishing channels. Some well established varieties like books and journals may be taken out of the purview of GL and for other varieties, special efforts may be made to achieve bibliographical control. There is a need to updating the assigned databases to the participating institutions in the standard formats, take into consideration the issues related to copy right, proprietary rights, licensing and security of information . To make sure that all the listed documents are available at the location. Methods may be developed for the cataloguing classification and indexing suiting to the international standards. There is a lot of potential for systematic research in this area.

Bibliography and References

Adams, Ralph. (1975) : Putting the minds of social scientists together : Towards a world social science information system. *International Social Science Journal*, 27(3), 519-31p.

________________ (1971) : Social science information and its users. *Journal of Librarianship*, 3,150-57 p.

Adiseshiah, Malcom S. (1983) : Uni,multi and interdisciplines in the social sciences. *ICSSR Newsletter*, 14(1), 1-12p.

Adisheshiah, M. Social Sciences in India (n.d) : 2 vols. Delhi : ICSSR.

Agrawal, S.P. (1987) : Social science information and documentation : Search for relevance in India. Delhi : Concept

________________ (1985) : Social science research institutions in India. *CLIS Observer*, 2(3-4), 7-14p.

Ahmed Sultan and Ranga Raja Rao (1983) : Generation, storage, retention and accessibility to GL in the National Laboratories. *In* Proceedings of the 14th IASLIC Conference, (New Delhi, 1982). Calcutta : IASLIC.

Aina, L.O (1987) : Grey Lliterature in Agricultural Research in Nigeria. *Quarterly Bulletin of the International Association of Agricultural Librarians and Documentalists*, 32(1), 48-50p.

________________ (1992) : Accession to development literature in Botswana. *Information Development*, 8(2), 104-108p.

________________ (94) : the problems of organising and disseminating of GL in Africa : *In* Proceedings of the Ist International Conference on Grey Literature.(

Amesterdam, 1993).Amesterdam : TransAtlantic.

————— (1996) : Promoting the exploitation of grey literature in Africa. *In* Proceedings of the 2nd Inter9national Conference on Grey Literature. (Washington D.C, 1995) . Amsterdam : TransAtlantic

Alberani Vilma, De Castro Pietrangeli Paola, Rossi Mazza Anna Maria (1990) : The use of Grey Literature in health sciences: A preliminary survey. *Bull.Med.Libr.Assoc.* 78(4), 358-363p.

Alberani, V. (1994) : Considerations on the organisational approach and treatment of grey literature in Italy. *In* Proceedings of the Ist International Conference on Grey Literature. (Amsterdam, 1993) . Amsterdam : TransAtlantic, 42-49p.

Alien, T.J (1969) : Information needs and uses. *Annual Review of Information Science and Technology,* 4, 3-29p.

Allison, P (1987) : Stalking the elusive GL. *College and Research Libraries News.* 48 (5), 244-246p.

Ambrose, D.P (1984) : The collection and bibliographic control of grey literature of Lesotho (Mimeo) Amesterdam : North-Holland.

Anthony, L.J ed. (1982) : Handbook of special Librarianship and Information work.5th ed. London: ASLIB.

Artus, H.M (84) : GL as a medium for scientific communication. Journal of Documentation., 35 (3), 139-141p.

Auger, C.P (1998) : Information sources in grey literature, 4th ed, London : Bowker- Saur.

—————(1989) : Information sources in grey literature, 2nd ed, London : Bowker- Saur.

—————(1978) : Information sources in Grey Literature, 3rd ed. London : Bowker- Saur.

————— (1982) : Non-Conventional literature : Chairman's introduction. *Aslib proceedings,* 34 (11/12), 457-458p.

______________ (1994) : Grey Literature establishing a clear identity. *In* Proceedings of the Ist Interantional Conference on Grey Literature. (Amsterdam, 1983)). Amesterdam : TransAtlantic

B.R.Ambedkar Open University (1998) : Information and Communication and Society , MLS-01. Hyderabad; Dr. B.R.Ambedkar Open University. (Course Material)

Barnabas, A.P (1981) : Social Sciences and development in the 1980s: Some issues. *Administrative Change*, 8, 210-214p.

Bath University. (1971) : Information requirements of Researches in Social Sciences. London : University of Bath,. (INFROSS Research Report No.1)

Batten WE.(ed). (1975) : Handbook of special librarianship and information work. London: ASLIB..

Beard, Charles A (1934) : Nature of Social Sciences. New York : Charles Scribner.

Bergen, Dan .(1966) : Bibliographic Organisation in the social sciences. *Wilson Library Bulletin*, 40 751-58.

Bernier, G (85) : Laws on access to administrative Information. *Documentation and Bibliothique*, 31 (2), 67-71p.

______________ (96) : Literature and para publications. *Documentaion Bibliothique*, 42 (1), 37p.

Britain, J.M and S.A. Roberts (1976) : Information Sources in the social sciences:Development and Rationalization. *International Social Science Journal*, 28(4), 835-40p.

Broadus, Robert N. (1971) :The Literature of Social Sciences. A survey of citation studies. *International Social Science Journal*, 23 (2), 236-43p.

Carbonnier and Marianne (83) : Tracts and the service for sources on the history of France. *Bulletin of Iformation of ASS of Bibliothque Francies*, 121 (4th quarter), 15-17p.

Carroll, B.C and Cotter, G.A (1993) : A new generation of GL : The impact of advanced Information Technologies. *In* Ist International Conference on GL, (Amesterdam, 1993) Amesterdam : TransAtlantic, 5-17p.

Chillag, J. (1982) : Non-Conventional literature in agriculture- an overview. *IAALD quarterly Bulletin,* 27(1), 2-7p.

Ching-Chih Chen (1982) : Information seeking : Assessing and anticipating user needs.New York : Neal-Schuman

Cleare, G.E (1996) Project management in GL : A study based on the development of the working papers project at the university of warwick._In Proceedings of the 2 nd International Conference on GL, (Washington D.C, 1995). Amesterdam : TransAtlantic.

Crawford, Susan (1978) : Information needs and users. *Annual review of Information Science and Technology,* 13, 61-81p.

Dasgupta, A.K (1983) : Indian Socio-economic development literature: enhancing accessibility to the grey variety. *In* 14th IASLIC Conference, (New Delhi,1982). Calcutta : IASLIC, 91-110p.

Datta, Amlan (1971) : What is wrong with social sciences in India? *ICSSR Newsletter* 3(1), 3-5p.

Datta, Bhabatosh (1990) : Social science research: Universities and autonomous institutions. *Journal of Higher Education* ,6(1-3), 15-24p.

Dbachere, M.C (1995) : Problems in obtaining Grey Literature. *IFLA Journal,* 21 (2), 94-98p.

Derr, R.L. (1984) : Information seeking expressions of users. *Journal of the American Society for Information Science,* 35, 124-28p.

Devadason, F.J and Lingam, P.P (1997). A methodology for the identification of information needs of users. *IFLA journal,* volume 27

DEVSIS (1976) : Preliminary design of an International Information System. Ottawa: IDRC.

Di cesare R and Sala, C (1993) : Use of grey literature in the agricultural economics field: A quantitive analysis. *In* Proceedings of the 2 nd. International Conference on GL, (Washington D.C, 1995). Amesterdam : Transatlantic.

Duverger, Maurice (1964) : Introduction to the social sciences. London : George Allen & Unwin.

Earle, P. and B.Vickery (1969) : Social Science Literature Use on the U.K. as indicated by Citation. *Journal of Documentation*, 25, 123-41p.

Encyclopedia of information and library science (1997) : Ed. by J. Feather and P Sturges. London : Routledge, 156p.

European Association For Grey Literature Exploitation (EAGLE) (1991) : SIGLE Manual 2 parts. 3rd. ed.. Den Haag : EAGLE.

Frieds, Thelma. (1982) : The State of Secondary Access Services : Social Sciences. *Journal of the American Society for Information Society*,33,157-61p.

Ganguly, S.M(1983) : Availability and use of official publications in libraries. *In* Proceedings of the 14th IASLIC Conference, (New Delhi ,1982). Calcutta : IASLIC.

Garfield, E (1985) : Society's unmet information needs. *Bulletin of the American Society for Information Science*, 12, 6-7p.

Garg, B.S (1974) : Natural sciences and social sciences : A comparative study. *Library Herald*, 16 (1-2), 48-62p.

Gelfand, J.M (1998) : Teaching and exposing Grey Literature : What the information profession needs to know, examples from the sciences. *Collection Building*, 17 (4), 159-66p.

———————— (97) : Academic libraries and collection development implication for GL. *Publishing Research Quarterly*, 13 (2), 15-23p.

Gibb J.M, Phillips E. (1979) : A better fate for the grey, or non-conventional literature. *Journal of Research Communication Studies*, 1, 225-234p.

Girija Kumar (1984) : Information needs of social sciences in India : A user education perspective. *In* Seminar on new perspectives in the meeting of Library Information Objectives held at Kuala Lumpur.

Goede, M.J.de. (1993) : Current Research Information in Europe.

In Proceedings of the Ist International Conference on GL (Amesterdam, 1993). Amsterdam : Transatlantic.

Goil, N.K. (1975) : Need for a social science information system : Guidelines for a model for India. *Library Herald* , 17(1-4), 70-93p.

Goil, N.K.(1979) : Social science information system in India: Proposed model. *In* IASLIC special publication 17, 249-60p.

Gokhale, P.A (1999) : Information system for grey literature in India : A model. *Library Science with Slant to Documentation and Information Science*, 36(4), 229-236p.

Goldberg, Aleksandr L.(1971) : Information needs of social scientists and ways of meeting them. *International Social Science Journal*, 23, 273-284p.

Gopal, M.H. (1979) : Criteria for Assesing Current Research in social sciences in Indian Universities. *Indian Economic Journal*, 32 (4), 70-93p.

Guttsman, W.L.(1966) : The Literature of the social sciences and provision of Research in them. *Journal of Documentation*, 22 (3), 184-94p.

Hanada, T (1984) : Grey Literature, its variety and problems. *Journal of Information Processing and Management*, 27(7), 595-602p.

Hayashi, S (1998) : Grey Literature in Japan. *Pharmaceutical Library Bulletin*, 43(3), 277-83p.

Herring, Pendalton (1970) : Development of social science research in India, ICSSR Occasional Monograph, no. 3 . New Delhi : ICSSR.

Hogeweg-De-Hart, H.P. (1984) : Characterstics of social science information: A selective review of literature. *Social Science Information Studies*, 4, 15-30p.

Holland, M (1989) : Times past and times to come . *World Wide Activities of Research Publications Serials*, 2(1), 49-50p.

Howard, T.W (1993) : Electronic Distribution of Hypermedia

on Wide-Area Networking Systems : An Update. *Technical Communication.* 438-448p.

Indian Council of Social Science Research (1978) : Report of the Review Committee on Social Sciences in India. Retrospective and Prospective.. New Delhi : ICSSR.

Indian Institute of Advanced study (1976) : Social Sciences and Social Relatives : Role of the Social Sciences in Contemporary India : Shimla..

Indian National Bibliography. Central Reference Library. New York : H.W. Wilson.

Institute of Economic Growth (1982) : Relevance in Social Science Research: A colloquium. New Delhi : Vikas. xv,374p.

International Development Research Centre : DEVSIS (1975) : The preliminary design of an international information system for the development science. Ottawa : IDRC.

International Encyclopaedia of Social Sciences (1954) : New York : Macmillan.

Joshi, P.C. (1981) : Some basic issues of social science research and the role of research institutes. *ICSSR Newsletter,* 12(1), 22-34p.

————— (1982) : Social Science Research and the Institutes . *Journal of Higher Education.* 8, 155-165p.

Kabamba, J.M. (1986) : Documentation of non-conventional literature in Africa. Problems and prospects. A masters dissertation.London : Loughborough University of Technology.

Kaula, P.N and Singh,S.N (1980) : Characteristics of information material : A bibliometric investigation in the field of social sciences in India. *Herald of Library Science,* 19,288-97p.

Keriguy, J (1984) : Access to Grey Literature : the contribution of the CNRS Centre for Scientific and Technical Documentation. *Bulletin-des-Bibliotheques-de-France,* 29 (2), 138-143p.

Khanna, J.K and Vishisht, K.K. (1985) : Landmarks and Research

Trends in Humanities and Social sciences. New Delhi : ESS ESS pub, 71-134p.

Kluck, Michael, M.A (1993) : The importance of Social Science Literature as a park of grey literature and the representation of social sciences in SIGLE. *In* Proceedings of the Ist International Conference on GL. (Amesterdam, 1993) . Amesterdam : TransAtlantic..

Kolby, Rober and Morris A. Geefend. Eds. (1974) : Access to the Literature of the social sciences and Humanities. New York : Queens college press.

Kreitz, P.A and others. (1995) : A virtual library in action : collaborative international control of high-energy pre-prints, *In* Proceedings of the 2nd. International Conference on Grey Literature, Washington D.C, (1995). Amesterdam : Trans Atlantic

Krishna Kumar,(1973) : Research Libraries in the Developing Countries. Delhi: Vikas.

Kwafo-Akoto, K. (1988) : Acquiring unpublished population documents in Africa : A personal experience. *ASLIB proceedings*, 40 (4), 105-110p.

Kwarfo-Akoto(1993) : GL and the DEVISIS project, the case of the National Institute of Research and Documentation Centre, University of Botswana. *In* Proceedings of the Ist International Conference on GL.(Amesterdam, 1993) Amesterdam : Trans Atlantic

Lahari, A (1997) : Libraries and Information Services : South Asia in World Information Report 1997-98. Paris : UNESCO.

Levin, M.A (1989) : The grey ghetto : Key issues related to public policy research literature. *Collection Building*, 10(1-2), 29.33p.

Line, M B. (1971) : The Information uses and needs of Social Scientists : An overview of INFROSS. *Aslib proceedings*, 23, 166-171 p.

——————— (1968) : Social Scientists Information. *Social*

Science Research Newsletter 3, 2-5p.

Luzi, D (1993) : The incidence of GL in on-line database, a quantitative analysis. *In* Proceedings of the Ist International conference on GL.(Amesterdam, 1993) Amesterdam : Trans Atlantic .

Luzi, D and Molinas, P (1987) : AGRIS, INIS, COSAT, SIGLE. *Bulletin of Information*, 27 (3-4), 325-344p.

Mackenzie and Owen, J. S (1997) : Value and use of GL : The implications of networked publishing. *In* Proceedings of the 3rd International Conference on GL.(Luxembourg, 1997). Amesterdam : TransAtlantic. 308-318p.

Madan, T.N. (1979) : Indegenization of social sciences. *ICSSR Newsletter*, 10 (1), 1-11p.

Mainieri, R (1987) : Grey Literature in the Italian ministries : Production, bibliographical control and availability. *Bulletin of Information* , 27 (3-4), 415-421p.

Marjorie L. I. (1998) : Access to Multicultural/Multiethinic Grey Literature : A networked Approach . *In* Proceedings of the 3rd International Conference on GL. .(Luxembourg, 1997). Amesterdam: TransAtlantic

McDermott, J.C. (1996) : Defining Grey Literature for the 21st Century. *In* Proceedings of the 2nd. International Conference on Grey Literature, Washington D.C .Amsterdam: TransAtlantic, 9-17p.

Moeshoe, M.M.M. (1985) : Grey Literature relating to Southern Africa: problems of definition, acquisition and handling. London,: University college of London.

Namjoshi, M.V. (1978) : Priorities in Social Science Research. *New Quest*, 83-93p.

Neeley, James D (1981) : The Management and social science Literature: An interdisciplinary Creoss-citation Analysis. *Journal of American Society for Information Science*,.32(3), 217-223p.

Norton, T (1983) : Grey Literature. *State Librarian* , 31(2), 16-17p.

Obikeze, D.S. (1979) : New approach to social research in Africa : The exchange process. *International Social Science Journal*, 31, 732-740p.

Ojo-Igbinoba, M.E (1997) : The potentials of internet for library services in Nigeria, *African journal of Library, Archives and Information Science*, 7(2), 91-104p.

Owen, J.M (1997) : The expanding of horizon of GL. *In* Proceedings of the 3rd International Conference on GL.(Luxembourg, 1997). Amesterdam : TransAtlantic. 308-318p.

Owm, JS (1993) : Value and use of grey literature : The implications of networking publishing. *In* Proceedings of the Ist International Conference on GL.(Amesterdam,1993) . Amesterdam : TransAtlantic..

Oxford Encyclopedic English Dictionary : (1991) .Oxford : Clarendon press, 622p.

Oxford English Dictionary. (1989) : 2nd ed..Oxford : Clarendon Press, 791p.

Paisley, W (1966) : Information needs and uses. *A Review of Information Science and Technology*, 3, 1-30p.

Palnikov, M.S, (1989) : Small circulation (Grey) literature in the institute of information in social sciences of the USSR. Academy of Sciences. *Inter lending and Document Supply*, 17(1), 16-19p.

Pandurangam, S.(1982) : Trade Literature in Industrial and Technical information centers. . *In* Proceedings of the 14th IASLIC Conference,(New Delhi, 1982). Calcutta : IASLIC.

Parekh, Harsha (1982) :Social Science Literature, Size, Use patterns and bibliographical services. *Economic and Political Weekly*,17(35), 1423-1428p.

Pathak, Vijay and L.S Ramaiah (1986) : Bibliography of Research in Library and information science in India. Gurgaon : Indian Documentation Service.

Peach, M (1998) : Archiving the internet web pages of political parties. *Assignation* ,15 (4) , 8-54p.

Popper Karl, R (1969) : Conjectures and Refutations: the growth of Scientific Knowledge. London : Routledge.

Posnett & Reilly, P.M (1986) : Non-Conventional literature in tropical agricultural & National Agricultural Bibliography an assessment. *Quarterly Bull. of the International Association of Agricultural Libraries & Documentalists,* 31(1), 27-33p.

Posnett and Baulkwill, (1982) : Working with Non-conventional Literature. *Journal of Information Science.* 15, 121-130p.

Posnett N.W and Baulkwill W.J (1982) : Working with Non-conventional Literature. *Journal of Information Science,* 5(4), 121-130p.

Posnett, N.W (1984) : Factors effecting the accessibility of non-conventional literature to use in U.K and some possible solutions, *Library Acquisitions: Practice and theory* 8(4), 275-285p.

Rab, S.F. (1994) : The changing frontiers of Library and Information Science, concepts, models and applications. New Delhi. : Commonwealth publishers.

Raben, J and G.Marks eds. (1980) : Data bases in the Humanities and Social Sciences. Amsterdam: North Holland.

Raj, K.N (1983) : Social Scientists and Social Revolution. *Mainstream,* 9(10), 12p.

Raju, A.A..N. (1971) : Social Science documentation in India. *IASLIC Bulletin* , 16 (4), 4-28p.

Raju, K.A and Satish, N.G(1982) : Bibliographic control of grey development literature with special reference to government documents_. *In* Proceedings of the 14th IASLIC Conference,(New Delhi, 1982). Calcutta : IASLIC.

Raju, K.A and Satish, N.G.. (1982) Towards understanding the information needs of development scientists: A case study._*In* Proceedings of the 10th. IASLIC National Seminar, (Kanpur, 1978). Calcutta : IASLIC..

Ramadevi, T (1988) : Use of grey literature in doctoral dissertations of the ANGR Agricultural University (1982-88). MLISc. Dissertation. Waltair :Andhra University, 85p.

Rama Reddy, E.(1985) : Social Science Information : Some Indian Sources. New Delhi : Affiliated East-West Press.

Ramaiah, L.S (1979) : Library and information work: a refresher course, April 9-23.Hyderabad : Academy of Library Science and Documentation.(Course Material)

——————— (1996) : Library and Information Science in India: Glimpses and Reflections. Delhi; ESS ESS pub.

Ranganathan, S.R. and Girija Kumar (ed) (1959) : Social Science Research and Libraries Asia : Bombay.

Rao, V.K.R.V.(1982) : Problems of relevance in social science research. *In* Relevance in Social Science Research .New Delhi : Institute of Economic Growth, 109p.

Raseroka, H.K (1986) : Relevant library services in developing countries. *IFLA Journal,* 12(4), 288-291p.

Rathapo, S.B.(1998) : Grey Literature on Women and Gender in Botswana. *Information Development,* 14 (3), 144-51p.

Roberts, N. Ed. (1977) : Use of Social Sciences Literature. London : Butterworth,

Roberts, S.A (1984) : Management and Development of Information and Library provision in the social sciences. *Journal of Documentation,* 40, 94-119p.

Roberts, Stepen (1976) : The size, growth and composition of social science literature. *International Social Science Journal,* 28 (1), 26-29p.

Rosa Di Cesare (1993) : The impact evaluation of GL impact in physical sciences using bibliometric indicators preliminary results. *In* Proceedings of the Ist International Conference on GL.(Amesterdam,1993) . Amesterdam : TransAtlantic..

Sahai, Shrinath (1979) : Use of information in the literature of sociology : A study of citation patterns. *Annals of Library Science and Documentation* , 26, 107-13p.

Sardana, J.L. (1977) : Social Science documentation in India. *Journal of Library and Information Science*, 2(1), 51-68p.

Satyanarayan, V.V.V. (1983) : Sources of generation and distribution of grey literature and its importance to research and development activities.. *In* Proceedings of the 14th IASLIC Conference,(New Delhi, 1982). Calcutta : IASLIC.

Schidmaier, D. (1986) : Ask no questions and you will be told no lies: or how we can remove people's fear of "Grey Literature". *Libri* ,36(2), 98-112p.

Seetharambai, N (1982) : GL as an information source in development finance institutions. *In* Proceedings of the 14th IASLIC Conference,(New Delhi, 1982). Calcutta : IASLIC

Seligman Edwin, R.a (1957) : what are social sciences ? Encyclopaedia of the social sciences. New York : Macmillan.

Sethi, A.R.(1982) : Bibliographical control of Indian publications in English. *ILA Bulletin* , 18 (1-2), 14-23p.

Sethi, A.R.(1990) : Information Seeking Behaviour of Social Scientists, an Indian conspectus. Delhi : Hindustan Publishers, xiii, 238p.

Shambhu Narayana Singh (1984) : Use of Social Science Literature in India. Varanasi: Banaras Hindu University. (ph.D. thesis)

Sheleton, Barbara. (1973) : Scientists and social scientists as information users : A comparison of results of science Users studies with the Investigation into Information requirements of the Social sciences. *Journal of Librarianship*. 5 (2), 138-156p.

Singh, K.K (1972) : Growth of Social Science Research in India : Issues and prospects. *ICSSR Newsletter,* 3 (2), 3-8p.

Smith, Natalia and Helen R. Tibbo. (1996) : Libraries and the Creation of electronic texts for the humanities. *College and Research Libraries*, 57(6), 535-553p.

Special Libraries Organisation, Research and Development, Library and Information Services, MLS-07. Hyderabad; Dr. B.R.Ambedkar Open University, 1985 and 1999. (Course Material)

Srivastav and Ajay Kumar(1982) : Towards improving accessibility of GL on Anthropology of India. . *In* Proceedings of the 14th IASLIC Conference,(New Delhi, 1982). Calcutta : IASLIC.

Stone, S. (1982) : Humanities scholars: Information needs and users. *Journal of Documentation*, 38, 292-313p.

Subramanyam, T. (1983) : Study of information seeking behaviour of doctoral candidates in social sciences. *Herald of Library Science*, 22, 200-204p.

Surdesai, D.B. (1973) : Social Science Data Archives : Emergence a New Institutions in India. *Artha Vijnana*, 15(4), 383-390p.

Suri, B.K.(1976) : Social Science Information. *Herald of Library Science*, 15(2), 106-111p.

Thielemann, J. (1986) : Grey official publications. *Bibliotek*, 53(2), 88-90p.

Thorpe, P (1985) : Priorities in information management for strengthening National Agricultural research. *Association of Agricultural Libraries and Documentalists*, 30 (4), 77-84p.

Tim Berners-Lee, et-al, (1992) : World-Wide web: The Information Universe. *Electronic Networking*, l2 , 52-58p.

Tyagi, K.G. (1999) : Information support Development studies. *DESIDOC Bulletin of Information Technology*, 18(4), 9-19p.

Van-der-Meer, K (1987) : The future of information resources for science and technology and the role of the library. Sweden : IATUL.

Ved Bhushan and Vyas, S.D. (1974) : Social Science Information System. *Herald of library Science*, 13(2), 116-123p.

Vender Heij (1985): Synopsis publishing for improving the accessibility of grey scholarly. *Journal of Iinformation Science*, 11, 95-107p.

Vickers, S and Wood, D.N (1982) : Improving the availability of Grey Literature. *Interlending Review*, 10(4), 125-130p.

Walsh V. (1997) : The future of the library profession. *IFLA Journal*, 23.

Weiner, Myron (1979) : Social Science Research and public policy in India. *Economic and Political Weekly*, 14(37), 1579-1587 .

White, Carl M. (1973) : Sources of information in the social sciences: a guide to literature, 2nd ed. Chicago : American Library Association.

Wilson (1964) : A communication perspective. Newbury park CA : Sage Publications.

Wood, D.N (1984) : Collection, Bibliographical Control, Access. *IFLA Journal*, 10(3), 278-283p.

Wood, D.N and Bower, C.N. (1969) : The Use of Social Science Literature . *Journal of Documentation*, 25(2), 69p.

Wood, David. (1982) : The role of British Library Lending Division. *Aslib proceedings*, 34 (11/12, 459-65p.

Yogendra Singh (1976) : Role of Social Sciences in India : a sociology of knowledge. *In* Social Sciences and Social Realities. Simla : Indian Institute of Advanced Study. 51-61p.

—————— (1982) : Relevance of social sciences in India: Some reflections. *In* Relevance in Social Science Research. New Delhi: Institute of Economic Growth, 25-43p.

Annexure - A
Profiles of Institutions

1.National Institute of Rural Development (NIRD)

The mission of NIRD is to facilitate rural development vigorously through governmental and non-governmental initiatives. NIRD is the country's apex body for undertaking training, research, action research and constancy functions in the rural development sector. It works as an autonomous organisation, supported by the Ministry of Rural Development, Government of India.

The institute's services are available to different ministries/departments of the Central and State Governments, banking institutions, public and private sector undertakings, voluntary bodies, non-governmental organisations and international agencies concerned with rural development.

NIRD has a 100,strong, Multi-disciplinary faculty belonging to 17 Centres; who are established specialists, trainers, researchers and consultants with proven credentials and long years of experience in their respective areas of specialisation.

Training is a major activity of the Institute. NIRD has a wide range of expertise and excellent infrastructure to train senior officers and executives in policy formulations management and implementation, of rural development; programmes. Over 150 programmes are offered every year. Besides Institute conducts several international training programmes to share with the Afro-Asian and Latin-American countries the rich Indian experience in managing rural development. About 3000 trainees pass through its portals annually.

Research and Action Research

The Institute undertakes empirical studies on identified themes viz. Rural Change, Socio-Economic and Human Development, Decentralisation, Rural Technology and Environmental Concerns, to assess the impact of rural development schemes, identify new areas for policy interventions and determine training needs. Another important activity is Action Research, which is location-specific in its nature and scope where an assumed model/theme is given a fair trial.

The consultancy services of the Institute are made available to national and international organisations. NIRD has consultancy, arrangements with UNDP, UNICEF, UNESCO, WHO, ILO, World Bank, ESCAP, CIRDAP, AARRO and, others.

Information Dissemination

The Institute disseminates the results of the research studies and recommendations of its various seminars and workshops through a number of publications. It brings out a quarterly Journal of Rural Development and a half-yearly, Grameen Vikas Sameeksha in Hindi and a monthly NIRD Newsletter - in English and Hindi. To bridge the gap at the Panchayat Level, NIRD publishes a monthly newsletter 'Grameen Bharat' in twelve major Indian languages and circulates it among the 2.5 lakhs Panchayati Raj Institutions all over the country. With over 250 publications to date, NIRD is a leading publisher of Rural Development literature in India. "India Rural Development Report" an Indian Panchayati Report has attracted a great deal of attention of academics and policy planners.

Documentation

The Centre on Rural Documentation (CORD) of the institute acts as a referral and servicing agency for the rural development sector as a whole. It has a well-organised and rich library with a collection of about 90,000 volumes and subscribes to nearly 450 journals apart from several CDs and

Videos. The total database consisting of over 1,80,000 items is computerised for expeditious retrieval. It has operationalised a project on Computerised Library and Information Clearinghouse (CLIC) to systematically collect, document, repackage and disseminate information, (especially for the Grey Literature) using internet resources. CORD brings out two periodicals every month entitled CORD Index and Cord Abstracts. It conducts seminars and workshops on networking, awareness building for IT among social science librarians.

2.Centre For Economic and Social Studies (CESS)

The Centre for Economic and Social Studies (CESS) was established as an autonomous body registered under the Societies Act, in the year 1980, with the initiative of the State Government. Appreciating its role in the promotion of research and training, the Indian Council of Social Science Research (ICSSR) recognised it as a national institute in the year 1986 and included CESS in its network of institutions.

The Faculty is drawn from different disciplines of social sciences for conducting multi-disciplinery research. The areas of the research of the faculty covers wide range of issues of the economy and society

Thrust Areas Of Research

The Centre's research activity developed research expertise on Agriculture, Food Security, Poverty Alleviation & Unemployment, Environment and Sustainable Development, District Planning, Bovine & Dairy Development, Resettlement & Rehabilitation, Tax systems, Health Economics and State and Local Finances.

Commissioned Projects

The Centre has been receiving support from the Government of India and Government of Andhra Pradesh as well as International agencies for undertaking research studies. The studies have been sponsored by Ministry of Rural Development, Planning Commission, Reserve Bank of India, NABARD, Indian Council for Social Science Research, Ministry of Urban Development at the Central Level. At the State level various departments of Government of Andhra Pradesh including Department of Finance and Planning, Panchayat Raj, Agriculture and Irrigation Department and Tribal Welfare Department. The Centre has undertaken sponsored research from International Organisations such as Ford Foundation, The World Bank, UNICEF, Asian Development Bank, and the European Union.

Networking

The Centre maintains a close functional relations with ministries of Central and State Government and other research institutes. It actively collaborates with the World Bank, UNICEF, Ford Foundation, IDPAD, and other international agencies. The Centre provides policy inputs 'through various studies to the State Government particularly to the Finance and Planning Department, Rural Development, Irrigation and agriculture departments. The Centre has estimated the district-wise incidence of poverty and examined the levels of living at the micro-level. Based on the studies on poverty and unemployment, the Centre designed a programme for Employment Guarantee in Andhra Pradesh. It has designed a programme for the Rehabilitation of Project Affected Families which the government has implemented in several villages. Besides this, a number of other studies also contribute to policy formulations The faculty members of the Centre have served as members of various committees and study groups appointed by the Central and State governments.

Academic and Teaching Activities

The Centre has been recognised as a Centre for advanced research by Dr.B.R.Ambedkar Open University and the Osmania University. The University of Hyderabad recognised the Centre as a Research Centre for external registration for Ph.D. programmes. The Centre has evolved a unique teaching-cum-research programme leading to M.Phil and Ph.D in Development Studies. Both are part-time programmes, undertaken in collaboration with Dr. B. R.Ambedkar Open

University. A few research scholars are offered doctoral fellowships (salary protected and student fellowships) funded by the Indian Council of Social Science Research (ICSSR) as well as by the Centre.

3.Osmania University

Osmania University established in 1918 was named after its royal founder - His Exalted Highness Sir Mir Osman Ali Khan, Nizam VII. It was the first University in the country to have chosen to impart higher education through the medium of an Indian Language, i.e., Urdu, with the study of English as a compulsory subject. It was also the first University in India to start an evening college in 1950. Facilities were made available for the study of Sanskrit, Marathi, Telugu and Kannada languages also. Nawab Habibur Rahman Khan Sherwani, (later Nawab Sadar Yar Jung) was its first Vice-Chancellor.

It is the eighth oldest University in India, the third oldest in South India and the first in the erstwhile princely state of Hyderabad. As a preliminary step, a Bureau of Translation was set up to translate textbooks and other reference materials from English and other languages into Urdu. The Bureau did a commendable job by translating 387 books into Urdu.

The advent of Independence and integration of Hyderabad State with the Indian Union in 1948 had their impact on the functioning of the Osmania University also. One important change was the replacement of Urdu, first by Hindustani and later by English as the medium of instruction of the University in the year 1949. Osmania University is a multi-faculty, multi-campus, semi- residential and affiliating University with 953 Faculty members and 2,989 non-teaching staff on its rolls.

The University offers various Diplomas, Undergraduate, Post-graduate and research courses through a network of 21 constituent colleges, of which seven are located on the University Campus, six in the twin cities of Hyderabad and Secunderabad and eight district P.G. Colleges in five districts of Telangana region, namely, Ranga Reddy, Medak, Nizamabad,

Nalgonda and Mahboobnagar. Besides these colleges, the University has 474 colleges managed by Govt. of India, Govt. of Andhra Pradesh, and Private educational institutions (both aided and self-financing). The jurisdictional area of the University covers nearly 60,000 Kms., which has a population of nearly 20 million.

In addition to these colleges, the University has set up a number of research and training centres, and advanced centres of excellence in the emerging areas of human concern and social relevance. Centre for Distance Education also offers certain courses through Distance Mode for the benefit of those who cannot join regular colleges.

Teaching and research activities are carried out in the University through its eleven faculty wise viz.,

(i) Arts
(ii) Business Management
(iii) Commerce
(iv) Education
(viii) Oriental languages
(v) Engineering
(vi) Informatics
(vii) Law
(viii) Oriental languages
(ix) Science
(x) Social Sciences
(xi) Technology

4. National Institute of Small Industry Extension Training (NISIET)

NISIET was shifted to Hyderabad in 1962, and was registered as an autonomous society under the Public Societies Registration Act, and was renamed as the Small Industry Extension Training (SIET) Institute.

SIET as an institute of meritorious performance under its Centres of Excellence Scheme to extend aid. Subsequently, it was also accorded national status and SIET Institute became nisiet in the same year. Nisiet is a pioneer Institute in enterprise promotion. It is an organisation of the Ministry of Small Scale Industries, Government of India.

NISIET aim is to promote and modernisation small

industries through training, research, consultancy and information services. It concentrates on policy research on small industry, industrial planning and development, entrepreneurship and extension, other schemes relating to SME development. There are about 20 faculty members, conducting 75 training programmes per year. NISIET publishes a Monthly Bulletin, having a circulation of 8,000 including industries and business enterprises, universities, libraries, govt. depts, NGOs and VOs

The SENDOC is the highly specialised information centre in the field of small enterprises in India. It was established in 1971 under the aegies of the National Institute of Small Industry Training (SIET) Hyderabad. The SENDOC undertakes information activities as an integral component of SIET which aims at promoting four major areas such as small industry development, management, extension and information for development. Consequently, information is the main thrust of SENDOC.

It provides comprehensive documentation services both anticipatory documentation services and responsive documentation service. The former relates to such activities which are organised in anticipation of the needs of the clienteles by bringing out SENDOC Bulletin, SENDOC chronicle, Appropriate Technology Documentation Bulletin SDI, Status of Technology Report (ST) Economic Survey Reports (ES), SENDOC Library and Information Bulletin etc. on the other hand, the latter confines to such activities which are organised on the basis of enquiries, requests and demands of the clienteles such as Technical Enquiry Service (TE), Pre-Investment Studies (PIS), Document Copying Service etc.

5.National Institute of Agricultural Extension Management (MANAGE)

The National Institute of Agricultural Extension Management (MANAGE), is an apex level autonomous body set up in 1987 under the Ministry of Agriculture, Government of India. It has a mandate to assist the State Governments, the

Government of India and other public sector and voluntary organizations in effective management of their agricultural extension systems. MANAGE offers its services in Consultancy; Management Training; Management Education; Research; and Information & Documentation services.

Mission: Facilitating the acquisition of managerial and technical skills by Extension Officers, Managers, Scientists and Administrators in all sectors of agricultural economy to enable them to provide most effective support and services to Farmers and Fishermen for practicing Sustainable Agriculture.

MANAGE LAN Network

A 140 node structured cabling Local Area Network (LAN) has been established in MANAGE to cater the needs of all the officers, staff and students in the administrative building with an internal as well as external Messaging system and INTERNET facility under 6 KBPS Leased line connection.

Information Sources

The Library has also developed a rich collection of over 300 videos, relating to agriculture and allied aspects and management. Besides books, journals and videos the library has also been subscribing to a number of databases and multimedia management packages on CD-ROMS. A collection of about 250 CD-ROMs on various aspects of agriculture and management are maintained. Databases received on a regular basis include AGRIS from FAO, AGRICOLA of the US National Agriculture Library, TROPAG & RURAL from Royal Tropical institute, Netherlands, CABSAC, the Compact International Agricultural Research Library, EXIM and PROWESS and India Trades. Several interactive CD-ROMs have also been procured, some from the Harvard Business School, on management education which include packages on communication, negotiation, team building etc.

The Library has been computerised using LIBSYS and access to the library database is available on LAN making it possible for faculty to search the on-line Public Access

Catalogue of the Library's Computerized cataloguing system. The catalogue offers access to books, reports, journals, videos, CD-ROMs available and journal articles along with abstracts for most. These can be retrieved by author, title, subject, keywords, publishers, and through use of Boolean operators. Development of a database of books and articles scanned from current literature is an on-going activity of this centre. Articles, of interest to research and training activities at MANAGE, are abstracted and made available to Faculty through the OPAC.

Information services include literature search services, bibliographic services, based on in-house and CD-ROM databases and the Internet; Documentation: Disseminating information through products and services like MANAGE Bulletin, Extension Digest, Fountain among policy makers, scientists and extension managers; Current Awareness Service; Selective Dissemination of Information (SDI); and Inter-Library Loan Service.

6. Administrative Staff College of India (ASCI)

Administrative Staff College of India (ASCI) is a pioneer in post-experience management education in the country. The College was set up in 1956 at the initiative of the Indian Industry and government. So far provided management education through their programmes to over 48,000 middle and senior level managers from Indian and international corporate and government sectors.

ASCI provide a unique learning environment in the form of comfortable classrooms, well equipped library and computer centre, comfortable single air-conditioned accommodation and a beautiful campus.

ASCI publishing the following journals regularly

ASCI Journal of Management, Lectures and other publications ,Faculty Publications.

ASCI Training

General Management ,Agriculture & Rural Development

,Centre for Infrastructure Management Information Technology, Economics, Energy, Environment & Technology ,Finance Human Resource ,Marketing Operations Strategic Management, Social Services Continuing our effort to help practising managers in India upgrade their skills and prepare themselves for meeting the managerial challenges posed by integration of world markets, now offer an opportunity to acquire internationally recognised Management Degree and Certificates in collaboration with Manchester Business School and University ofWales, Bangor. All these programme combine the convenience of Distance Learning with advantages of regular faculty contact through workshops.

ASCI offering the following courses

MBA for Financial Management, Certificates in Business Administration, Corporate Programme, Library & Virtual Information Centre

ASCI Library is one of serials. The library is kept open for 12 hours a day . It is used exclusively by the Faculty and Programme the best management libraries in India. At present the library has a collection of over 65,000 books and several hundreds of back volumes in addition to about 350 journals and statistical participants. At present the library offers the following facilities:

* Reference Service,
* Database search services,
* Photocopy facilities.
* Internet services

The Library has launched a project for setting up Virtual Information Centre for Management Development. This Centre envisages to make available the Internet based information to the users and also to run several services cyber world has made possible. An electronic catalogue of library holdings is being networked with a campus wide local area network. Participants have an unlimited access to the Internet.

7.Indian Institute of Public Enterprise (IPE)

The Institute of Public Enterprise (IPE), Hyderabad is a registered non-profit educational Society which is supported by the Indian Council of Social Science Research and the Government of Andhra Pradesh. It was established in 1964 at the initiative of the then Cabinet Secretary to the Govt. of India and Osmania University to promote, encourage and support research in public systems and administrative management sciences. It has since developed over the years as a premier institute of research, consultancy, training, Information Technology, Bio-tech delivery systems and management education. It has a strong faculty and an eminent quest faculty. IPE is an acknowledged Centre of Excellence in Public Sector studies and business management. In fact IPE is now the only institute of its kind in the whole of south-east Asia and perhaps in the world, exclusively devoted to public sector enterprise studies and management. This is particularly pertinent because of the recent changes in the mandate of the International Centre for Public Enterprises (ICPE), Ljubjliana-which is no longer exclusively devoted to public enterprise studies

Research and Training Activities

The Institute has a strong research wing with a number of research scholars sponsored by ICSSR and IPE working on topics of current interest. Its Ph.D. programme is one of the largest in the social science field. The Institute is recognised as a training centre for conduct of training courses for the Central and State government officials and public sector executives.

Consultancy

IPE has undertaken consultancy work at international level besides participating in collaborative programmes with United Nations Development Programme, World Bank, Asian Development Bank, Commonwealth Secretariat, Overseas Development Agency (ODA), International Centre for Public Enterprise (ICPE), Asian and Pacific Development Centre, Kaula-Lumpur and Universities of London, Bradford and Leeds in U.K. It is currently engaged in a study on restructuring of state level public enterprises in a major state in India for an International Development Bank. IPE welcomes enquiries for consultancy and research studies.

Information Technology Division

IPE has a strong Information Technology Division manned by senior and experienced persons and specialises in training and software applications. The Computer Centre is provided with a central mini computer with 15 terminals and 50 pentium processor based PCs each with a capacity of IGB hard disk, 166 MHz, with 16 MB RAM with a CD ROM drive. IPE has been actively involved in designing, developing and implementing a number of information systems for various enterprises and government departments etc.

Educational Activities

IPE started the 3-year part-time MBA (PE) course in 1981, started as PGDBM equivalent to MBA with the approval of AICTE in 1995, IPE is the only institution in Andhra Pradesh linked to CAT examination. IPE conducts a full time one-year postgraduate diploma course in Software Engineering (PGDSE). IPE is probably now the only Institute in Hyderabad to have received the 'C' level provisional accreditation.

Linkages with Government, Corporate and Academic Institutions

The Institute has close academic links at the national level with the Planning Commission, Department of Public Enterprise of the Government of India, Government of Andhra Pradesh, and other State Governments, Indian Council of Social Science Research (ICSSR), Standing Conference of Public Enterprises (SCOPE), Administrative Staff College of India.

Library

The Institute's Library has a rich collection of 35,000 documents which includes, books, pamphlets and journal bound volumes organised as per the Dewey Decimal

Classification in IPE related broad subject areas with classification numbers. The library collection includes the publication of the Comptroller and Auditor General (CAG), Government of India, the Annual Survey of Public Enterprise brought out by the Ministry of Industry, Government of India and also the evaluation reports brought by the different State Bureau of Public Enterprises

8. Acharya N.G Ranga Agricultural University

The Andhra Pradesh Agricultural University established in 1964 on the lines of Land Grant Universities pattern of USA extends its jurisdiction to the entire State of Andhra Pradesh and has a mandate for teaching, research and extension in agriculture and allied subjects. It has three Agricultural Colleges located at Hyderabad, Bapatla and Tirupati, two Colleges of Veterinary Science at Hyderabad and Tirupati and two Colleges of Home Science at Hyderabad and Bapatla besides the Extension Education Institute at Hyderabad and 56 Research stations scattered all over the State. The University has an-intake of 1000 students in the faculties of agriculture, Veterinary Science and Home Science. Till 1979 the libraries of the constituent Colleges used to cater to the needs of mainly students and teachers. In 1980 the APAU library systm has been reorganised forming the Central Library at Rajendranagar and Regional Libraries at Tirupati and Bapatla.

The library system together has a collection of over 200 thousands of books and subscribes to over 500 periodcals. The central library exchanges 125 copies of ANGRAU Research journal to various National and international institutions. The regional agricultural stations have sizeable collection of books to meet the requirements of the scientists at the sub stations in the Zone.

In addition to normal services such as issue of books for home reading, reference service, orientation of readers etc. Separate book banks for economically backward class students, SC/ST students.

Documentation Work

Agricultural Information and Documentation Centre(Agridoc) located in the central library takes care of the information needs of the scientists at all the 67 university research stations in the state. The publications include Union Catalogue of periodicals in APAU libraries, Agricultural Dissertations Index/abstracts.Literature searches made available at Hyderabad, Tirupathi and Baptla. All the libraries are provided with personal computers and photocopy machines

9.University of Hyderabad

The University of Hyderabad, a premier institution of post-graduate teaching and research in the country, was established by an Act of Parliament on 2nd October, 1974 as a Central University, wholly financed by the University Grants Commission.The objectives of the university as envisaged in the Act are: "to disseminate and advance knowledge by providing instructional and research facilities in such branches of learning as it may deem fit and by the example of its corporate life, and, in particular, to make special provisions for integrated courses in humanities and science in the educational programmes of the University and to take appropriate measures for promoting inter-disciplinary studies and research in the University".

Schools of study

School of Mathematics and computer/information sciences.

School of physics

School of chemistry

School of life sciences

School of Humanities

School of social sciences

School of Management studies

School of Performing Arts, Fine Arts and communication

Over the years, the teaching and research programmes of the University have been firmly established. The students are selected through a nation-wide entrance test. Over 35% of the students consist of Ph.D scholars and 33% of the students are women. Till the VIII Convocation of the University held on March 4, 2000, the university has conferred 94404 Degrees and Diplomas through formal education including 677 Ph.Ds., 2009 M.Phils. 525 M.Techs and 6193 post-graduate Degrees and Diplomas. The faculty of the University includes 71 professors, 86 Readers and 42 lecturers. An Academic staff college has been functioning on the University campus since 1988 under the UGC scheme for improving the standards of teaching in colleges and Universities as part of the new Education and refresher courses for college and university teachers.

Indira Gandhi Memorial Library

University library is the central facility to support the teaching and research needs of the university. This library has the distinction of being the first university library in India to computerise all its activities and also provide computer terminals (OPAC) to the user with network access across the campus - wide local area (LAN).

The library collection includes 2,53,000 volumes and 670 current periodicals, over 50 popular magazines and 25 newspapers. Library has several CD-ROMs and multimedia products and they are used in training the users in handling these products. The reference collection in the library include directories, dictionaries, encyclopaedias, yearbooks, handbooks annual publication, maps, films, database products etc. All this material is not for circulation and available on computer as a database and they need to be consulted in the library. Photocopy facilities are available to the users on payment. Audio-visual facilities are also available in the library. Presently digitization of the library material is in progress.

Computer Centre

Most of the schools and departments of the University are networked through Ethernet to all the systems. The University of Hyderabad is connected to internet via VSAT. The computer center runs round the clock.

Index